The Dogma of Christ

'Fromm's *The Dogma of Christ* will perhaps be a title ignored by the anti-religious psychologist and social theorist, but it is the message hidden behind its title that provides some of the sharpest critical insights into how the contemporary world of human destructiveness and violence can no longer separate religion, psychology and politics. Erich Fromm today is a prophetic voice crying in the wilderness of neo-liberal ideology.'

Jeremy Carrette, University of Stirling

'Among the most widely read social theorists of his day, Dr. Fromm also was among the most prolific and eclectic of writers on the nature of man.'

The Washington Post

'Fromm crossed the boundaries of traditional disciplines to expound his views on the alienation of man in an increasingly technological world.'

Newsweek

Routledge Classics contains the very best of Routledge publishing over the past century or so, books that have, by popular consent, become established as classics in their field. Drawing on a fantastic heritage of innovative writing published by Routledge and its associated imprints, this series makes available in attractive, affordable form some of the most important works of modern times.

For a complete list of titles visit
www.routledgeclassics.com

Erich

Fromm

The Dogma of Christ

And other essays on religion, psychology and culture

With a new preface by Jeremy Carrette, University of Stirling

London and New York

First published 1963 by Routledge & Kegan Paul Limited, London

First published in Routledge Classics 2004
by Routledge
2 Park Square, Milton Park, Abingdon, Oxfordshire, OX14 4RN
711 Third Avenue, New York NY 10017

Routledge is an imprint of the Taylor & Francis Group, an informa business

Typeset in Joanna by RefineCatch Limited, Bungay, Suffolk

Index compiled by Indexing Specialists (UK) Ltd, Hove

British Library Cataloguing in Publication Data
A catalogue record for this book is available from the British Library

ISBN 10: 0-415-28999-8
ISBN 13: 978-0-415-28999-3

CONTENTS

Preface to the Routledge Classics Edition

Erich Fromm (1900–1980) is known in the history of psychology as bridging the links between Marx and Freud, emerging as he did from the Frankfurt School of Social Theory and carrying his work into the social climate of North American and Mexican culture. His theoretical acumen enabled him to raise fundamental questions about the nature of being human and to locate such questions in the political and economic conditions of his time. With his critical analysis of the contemporary world and his far-reaching insights into the restrictive nature of modern living, he raised the uncomfortable issue of whether the social shaping of the human being did justice to the creative potential of human life. With his unsettling analysis of the conditions of Western society, he was a voice for humanity in a world driven by its own destructive and aggressive impulses. His social critique, not surprisingly, carried forward his childhood fascination with the eighth-century Jewish prophets, Isaiah, Amos and Hosea. These voices of justice continued in the work of Karl Marx and allowed Fromm to establish an effective social critique that still holds a prophetic force.

The bringing together of religion, politics and psychology is perhaps an extraordinary register of the complexity of the problems facing the contemporary world. Where disciplinary paradigms may wish to separate these fields of study, Fromm shows it is necessary to rebuild the fragmented knowledge of a consumer culture. Politics, religion and psychology inter-related and depend on each other and it is only a naive system of knowledge that tries to separate these realms for a commercial or institutional rationale. Fromm recognised the problems of defining religion in his 1950 study *Psychoanalysis and Religion* and the inter-relation of different fields of study in this volume indicates his appreciation of this problem. There is a constant interaction between religious, social, psychological and political worlds, as they shape and reflect each other, and in many senses these categories collapse into each other. The problem in determining the reality of the psychological is that there is always something that exceeds the rational account and the very persistence of religion in an age of science shows that human beings constantly live with the perplexity of their own mysterious existence.

The Dogma of Christ is made up of eight essays from Fromm's work between 1930 and 1963, the largest and earliest of these – from which the volume intriguingly takes its name – reflects the critical and theoretical foundation through which Fromm links economics, politics and psychology inside the history of religious ideas. This enfolding of issues is Fromm's first sustained attempt to link Marx and Freud. While, as he indicates, this essay reflects a time when he was less critical of Freud's work, it shows the ground for his integrated project. *The Dogma of Christ* provides an insight into how Fromm developed the idea of "social character" and how he identified social class as an important factor in differentiating religious attitudes. It was in the interests of method and argument that Fromm agreed to republish such an early piece and we are rewarded from this point of view, even if the historical material on the church in late antiquity can now be updated. However, Fromm's study takes on renewed interest in the light of contemporary work in cultural theory and the examination of conceptions of the self in early Christian literature. Such re-examinations read history in terms of the regimes of power and recognise the importance of new ideas of the self produced in Christianity. As Judith Perkins in her study *The Suffering Self: Pain and Narrative Representation in the Early Christian Era* (Routledge, 1995: 11) has indicated, the "triumph of Christianity was, in part at least, a triumph of a particular representation of the self". Fromm's correlation of the production of dogma with the social structures of character is a critical direction that has yet to be fully appreciated. To locate the reified images and doctrines of Christianity inside the politics of knowledge is to transform theology and the study of religion. Fromm challenges Christian theologians to recognise "the psychic condition that roots them inwardly in an existing social situation" (11). It is such a uniting of the psyche, religious dogma and social structures that allows human beings to examine critically who they are within the limits of historical knowledge – something which is a hallmark of contemporary social theory.

The critical importance of Fromm's study for the history of psychology is its attempt to challenge the binary construction of the individual and social. This tension resides at the heart of psychological theory from its inception. It is also something that registers how the human being exceeds the methods of natural science (154). Fromm marks out the basis of the "false distinction" between social and individual reality and it is this that underlines the continuing importance of Fromm's work. The emergence of "critical psychology", since the crisis of social psychology in the 1970s, and the introduction of post-structuralism and critical theory into psychology, in the last 20 years, assert the importance of the political understanding of psychological knowledge. Fromm is not just recalling the foundational problems of psychology, which we find in Wilhelm Wundt's *Völkerpsychologie*, but heralding the work of French post-structuralist thinkers, such as Louis Althusser and Michel Foucault, who addressed the same problem in a different way, with the notion of "assujettissement" (subjectification), examining how the individual subject was constructed through social processes. Fromm is a "critical psychologist" before critical psychology and recognises the "limits" of psychology and its political context. As he writes in his essay 'On the Limitations and Dangers of Psychology' (1959), in this volume: "Psychological knowledge ("Menschenkenntniss") has assumed a particular function in capitalist society, a function and a meaning quite different from the meanings implied in 'Know Thyself' ". (157)

Fromm's recognition of the relationship between capitalism and psychology and the calls for a "negative psychology" to stand alongside a "negative theology" demonstrates how he attempts to preserve the mystery of being human from the reductive forces of the market (162).

To read Fromm's social critique in the context of the twenty-first century is not just some historical recollection of a social-psychological political thinker, it is rather to recognise that his diagnosis of society holds an even greater importance and an alarming relevance. The new publication of the essays in the collection *The Dogma of Christ*, some 40 years from its original publication in 1963, carries an even greater poignancy and power after the domination of neo-liberal ideology. While some of Fromm's questions still reflect the context of the Cold War and the sexual politics of liberal Americans in the 1960s, the broader issues still hold political and academic relevance. His work takes on even greater urgency after the machine of capitalism is given free reign in the era of Margaret Thatcher and Ronald Reagan in the United States and Britain. The psychological and political implications of reducing human beings to the market are already being recognised by Fromm. Grasping how the internal worlds of human beings are shaped by a social machine is the disturbing vision of Fromm's work. Today such work challenges us to reconsider ethically the implications of global capitalism in determining our sense of self.

The strength of Fromm's work is the way he recognises more than most the horrors of fascism, communism *and* capitalism. He realises that they all hold the dangers of creating human beings as "automatons" – machines in the services of ideological regimes. Fromm also uncomfortably shows that "democracy has become more and more influenced by the methods of manipulation which were first developed in market research and human relations" (159). Fromm rightly feared the slow invasion of market forces into every area of life and this insight takes on even more disturbing levels of truth today. He saw the way human beings were commodified and made into "things" in "managerial societies" (88). Something that takes on even more sinister levels of reductionism when "personnel departments" become "departments of human resources" in the institutions of the Western world. What Fromm saw in 1960s consumer culture has now become an ever-greater prison of human experience. "Man [sic] has transformed *himself* [sic] into a commodity, and experiences his life as capital to be invested profitably; if he succeeds in this he is 'successful' and his life has meaning; if not, 'he is a failure'." (84)

The conformity of human values to the values of the market is, as Fromm realised, the destruction of "man". In Fromm's time it was boredom and meaninglessness that faced humanity now it is the "death of man", not simply in the post-structuralist sense, but the reduction of humanity to consuming machines (88). The control of society through fear and social disconnection creates a world where to live life "intensely and with zest" (149) is terrifying for people who are anxious about being separated from the numbing machine of media intoxication and the religion of money. As Fromm hints, it is not fear of death but fear of life that is the cause of suffering, each individual seeking a tranquilliser for all the problems of life (142). In the attempt to bring the Western world back from its exploitation, authoritarianism, inequality and stinginess (145–6), Fromm draws on the rich traditions of social justice held within religion. He highlights the failure of Christianity to carry out its radical social gospel for the poor, as it became part of the social hierarchy and mechanisms of conformity – such that today Christians consume for Christ and hide from the poverty such practices create. It is the move from Christianity as a "religion of the oppressed to the religion of the rulers" (54). The abuses of capitalism also extended into the very heart of dogma and religious symbols.

> We use symbols belonging to a genuinely religious tradition and transform them into formulas serving the purpose of alienated man. Religion has become an empty shell; it has been transformed into a self-help device for increasing one's own powers for success. God becomes a partner in business. (87)

This prognosis of religion in the age of capitalism becomes even more alarming with the rise of contemporary spirituality and its fusion with business and corporate society (see Carrette, J. and King, R. *Selling Spirituality: The Silent Takeover of Religion*, Routledge, 2004). Fromm's early sense of how religion was subverted in the market was a profound realisation of how alienated human beings had become inside the economic control of late capitalism. However, Fromm did not reject the roots of social justice in the religious traditions and it is perhaps significant that this collection of work ends with a series of reflections on the eighth-century Jewish prophets and the appeal to a 'Messianic time' of a new harmony. What is important for Fromm is the understanding of the Messiah as a symbol of the *human* struggle for justice (170). Fromm searches for a social, psychological and political "at-one-ment" in line with the prophets.

For some, it may be remarkable that a social-psychological thinker turns to the history of religion, but such a move is not simply a recognition of the significance of religion and psychological studies, but an understanding of the importance of such religious traditions to provide an ethical context for human society. Fromm, of course, was not restricted to Western traditions and in other work – and in passing here – he explored the importance of Zen Buddhism. These adventures into religious traditions reflect the need to find ways of thinking about being human outside both capitalism and psychology. It is to recognise that these practices are, in part at least, oppressive to human flourishing. The need to move beyond these frames of reference is the desire to find ways of overcoming the constraints being offered in the automated worlds of the market. Capitalism and psychology work together to make human beings into machines. If, as Fromm suggests, the danger of the nineteenth-century is becoming slaves and the danger of the twentieth-century is becoming robots, the danger of twentieth-century is losing the critical capacity to see we are becoming economic cyborgs. Fromm's *The Dogma of Christ* will perhaps be a title ignored by the anti-religious psychologist and social theorist, but it is the message hidden behind its title that provides some of the sharpest critical insights into how the contemporary world of human destructiveness and violence can no longer separate religion, psychology and politics. Erich Fromm today is a prophetic voice crying in the wilderness of neo-liberal ideology. He is someone who is not afraid to demand a new politics of life, love and justice in the face of an entrenched and destructive psychological and economic control of society. By returning to his texts it is possible to rediscover and imagine new ways of being human outside the oppressive ideologies of our time.

JEREMY CARRETTE
2004

Preface

While most of the essays in this volume have been written during the last ten years, the longest paper, "The Dogma of Christ", first appeared in German in 1930. Professor James Luther Adams of the Harvard Divinity School made a translation many years ago and suggested that I publish it together with other papers in one volume. He did so in spite of the fact that he was not in agreement with most of my conclusions. He felt, however, that the method and the argument were sufficiently interesting to warrant publication in English. I myself was very hesitant to reissue this early example of my thought. The reasons are obvious.

First of all, it was written in a period when I was a strict Freudian. In the meantime my psychoanalytic views have undergone enough of a change so that many formulations in this essay would be different if I wrote them today. A second reason lies in the fact that it is impossible for me today to restudy the whole of the rather complex historical material which is analysed in this work. A great number of books on the history of early Christianity have been published since 1930, and any revision of "The Dogma of Christ" would have to take them into account. I have read much of the literature in the intervening years and some, like Martin Werner's *The Formation of Christian Dogma*, seemed to give some indirect support to my approach; but a thorough rewriting would go beyond my powers. I agreed to the publication of the paper in its original form when Arthur Cohen of Holt, Rinehart and Winston, a scholar of theology and philosophy in his own right, urged me again, together with Professor Adams, to offer it to an English-reading audience. Needless to say, the responsibility for this decision lies with me and not with them. I decided on publication after thoroughly rereading "The Dogma of Christ", and I hope it may still prove of value.

As far as I know, this is the first work in which the attempt was made to transcend the psychologistic approach to historical and social phenomena so customary in psychoanalytic literature. I had been stimulated by the paper on the same subject written by one of my teachers at the Psychoanalytic Institute in Berlin, Dr. Theodor Reik, who had employed the traditional method. I tried to show that we cannot understand people by their ideas and ideologies; that we can understand ideas and ideologies only by understanding the people who created them and believed in them. In doing this we have to transcend individual psychology and enter the field of psychoanalytic-social psychology. Thus, in dealing with ideologies, we have to study the social and economic conditions of the people who accept them, and try to recognize what I later called their "social character".

The main emphasis of this study is the analysis of the socio-economic situation of the social groups which accepted and transmitted Christian teaching; it is only on the basis of this analysis that a psychoanalytic interpretation is attempted. Whatever the merits of this interpretation, the method of the application of psychoanalysis to historical phenomena is the one which has been developed in my subsequent books. While it has since been refined in many ways, its nucleus is contained in "The Dogma of Christ" in a way which, I hope, is still interesting.

I have gone over Professor Adams' translation and sympathize with the difficulty of translating my rather heavy, academic German into English. Here and there I have made minor changes in wording, but have consistently resisted the temptation to change the contents. Even though many times I would have liked to substitute my present point of view for the older one, a partial revision, I felt, would not have been fair to the reader.

The other papers do not need any lengthy comment. I have not attempted to revise those that have already appeared; in the paper on "Sex and Character", I have simply eliminated what seemed to me needless repetition.

I am greatly indebted to Professor James Luther Adams for his labour of love in translating "The Dogma of Christ", and to Arthur A. Cohen and Joseph Cunneen for their editorial assistance.

E.F.

New York, 1963

1

THE DOGMA OF CHRIST

1. METHODOLOGY AND THE NATURE OF THE PROBLEM

It is one of the essential accomplishments of psychoanalysis that it has done away with the false distinction between social psychology and individual psychology. On the one hand, Freud emphasized that there is no individual psychology of man isolated from his social environment, because an isolated man does not exist. Freud knew no *homo psychologicus*, no psychological Robinson Crusoe, like the economic man of classical economic theory. On the contrary, one of Freud's most important discoveries was the understanding of the psychological development of the individual's earliest social relations—those with his parents, brothers, and sisters.

"It is true", Freud wrote:

> that individual psychology is concerned with the individual man and explores the paths by which he seeks to find satisfaction

> for his instinctual impulses; but only rarely and under certain exceptional conditions is individual psychology in a position to disregard the relations of this individual to others. In the individual's mental life someone else is invariably involved, as a model, as an object, as a helper, as an opponent; and so from the very first individual psychology, in this extended but entirely justifiable sense of the words, is at the same time social psychology as well.[1]

On the other hand, Freud broke radically with the illusion of a social psychology whose object was "the group". For him, "social instinct" was not the object of psychology any more than isolated man was, since it was not an "original and elemental" instinct; rather, he saw "the beginning of the psyche's formation in a narrower circle, such as the family". He has shown that the psychological phenomena operative in the group are to be understood on the basis of the psychic mechanisms operative in the individual, not on the basis of a "group mind" as such.[2]

The difference between individual and social psychology is revealed to be a quantitative and not a qualitative one. Individual psychology takes into account all determinants that have affected the lot of the individual, and in this way arrives at a maximally

[1] *Group Psychology and the Analysis of the Ego* (Standard edition, XVIII), p. 69.

[2] Georg Simmel has strikingly indicated the fallacy of accepting the group as a "subject", as a psychological phenomenon. He says: "The unified external result of many subjective psychological processes is interpreted as a result of a unified psychological process—i.e., of a process in the collective soul. The unity of the resulting phenomenon is reflected in the presupposed unity of its psychological cause! The fallacy of this conclusion, however, upon which the whole of collective psychology depends in its general distinction from individual psychology, is obvious: the unity of collective actions, which appears only on the side of the visible result, is transferred surreptitiously to the side of the inner cause, the subjective bearer." "Über das Wesen der Sozialpsychologie", *Archiv für Sozialwissenschaft und Sozialpolitik*, XXVI, 1908.

complete picture of the individual's psychic structure. The more we extend the sphere of psychological investigation, that is, the greater the number of men whose common traits permit them to be grouped, the more we must reduce the extent of our examination of the total psychic structure of the individual members of the group.

The greater, therefore, the number of subjects of an investigation in social psychology, the narrower the insight into the total psychic structure of any individual within the group being studied. If this is not recognized, misunderstandings will easily arise in the evaluation of the results of such investigations. One expects to hear something about the psychic structure of the individual member of a group, but the social-psychological investigation can study only the character matrix common to all members of the group, and does not take into account the total character structure of a particular individual. The latter can never be the task of social psychology, and is possible only if an extensive knowledge of the individual's development is available. If, for example, in a social-psychological investigation it is asserted that a group changes from an aggressive-hostile attitude toward the father figure to a passive-submissive attitude, this assertion means something different from the same statement when made of an individual in an individual-psychological investigation. In the latter case, it means that this change is true of the individual's total attitude; in the former, it means that it represents an average characteristic common to all the members of the group, which does not necessarily play a central role in the character structure of each individual. The value of social-psychological investigation, therefore, cannot lie in the fact that we acquire from it a full insight into the psychic peculiarities of the individual members, but only in the fact that we can establish those common psychic tendencies that play a decisive role in their social development.

The overcoming of the theoretical opposition between

individual and social psychology accomplished by psychoanalysis leads to the judgment that the method of a social-psychological investigation can be essentially the same as the method which psychoanalysis applies in the investigation of the individual psyche. It will therefore be wise to consider briefly the essential features of this method, since it is of significance in the present study.

Freud proceeds from the view that in the causes producing neuroses—and the same holds for the instinctual structure of the healthy—an inherited sexual constitution and the events that have been experienced form a complementary series:

> At one end of the series stand those extreme cases concerning which you may say with confidence: These people would have fallen ill whatever happened, whatever they experienced, however merciful life had been to them because of their anomalous libido-development. At the other end stand cases which call forth the opposite verdict—they would undoubtedly have escaped illness if life had not put such and such burdens upon them. In the intermediate cases in the series, more or less of the disposing factor (the sexual constitution) is combined with less or more of the injurious impositions of life. Their sexual constitution would not have brought about their neurosis if they had not gone through such and such experiences, and life's vicissitudes would not have worked traumatically upon them if the libido had been otherwise constituted.[3]

For psychoanalysis, the constitutional element in the psychic structure of the healthy or of the ill person is a factor that must

[3] *A General Introduction to Psychoanalysis*, Garden City, N.Y., 1943, p. 304. Freud says "the two factors" are "sexual constitution and events experienced, or if you wish, fixation of libido and frustration"; they "are represented in such a way that where one of them predominates the other is proportionately less pronounced".

be observed in the psychological investigation of individuals, but it remains intangible. What psychoanalysis is concerned with is experience; the investigation of its influence on emotional development is its primary purpose. Psychoanalysis is aware, of course, that the emotional development of the individual is determined more or less by his constitution; this insight is a presupposition of psychoanalysis, but psychoanalysis itself is concerned exclusively with the investigation of the influence of the individual's life-situation on his emotional development. In practice this means that for the psychoanalytic method a maximum knowledge of the individual's history—mainly of his early childhood experiences but certainly not limited to them—is an essential pre-requisite. It studies the relation between a person's life pattern and the specific aspects of his emotional development. Without extensive information concerning the individual's life pattern, analysis is impossible. General observation reveals, of course, that certain typical expressions of behaviour will indicate typical life patterns. One could surmise corresponding patterns by analogy, but all such inferences would contain an element of uncertainty and would have limited scientific validity. The method of individual psychoanalysis is therefore a delicately "historical" method: the understanding of emotional development on the basis of knowledge of the individual's life history.

The method of applying psychoanalysis to groups cannot be different. The common psychic attitudes of the group members are to be understood only on the basis of their common patterns. Just as individual psychoanalytic psychology seeks to understand the individual emotional constellation, so social psychology can acquire an insight into the emotional structure of a group only by an exact knowledge of its life pattern. Social psychology can make assertions only concerning the psychic attitudes common to all; it therefore requires the knowledge of life situations common to all and characteristic for all.

If the method of social psychology is basically no different from that of individual psychology, there is, nevertheless, a difference which must be pointed out.

Whereas psychoanalytic research is concerned primarily with neurotic individuals, social-psychological research is concerned with groups of normal people.

The neurotic person is characterized by the fact that he has not succeeded in adjusting himself psychically to his real environment. Through the fixation of certain emotional impulses, of certain psychic mechanisms which at one time were appropriate and adequate, he comes into conflict with reality. The psychic structure of the neurotic is therefore almost entirely unintelligible without the knowledge of his early childhood experiences, for, owing to his neurosis—an expression of his lack of adjustment or of the particular range of infantile fixations—even his position as an adult is determined essentially by that childhood situation. Even for the normal person the experiences of early childhood are of decisive significance. His character, in the broadest sense, is determined by them, and without them it is unintelligible in its totality. But because he has adjusted himself psychically to reality in a higher degree than the neurotic, a much greater part of his psychic structure is understandable than in the case of the neurotic. Social psychology is concerned with normal people, upon whose psychic situation reality has an incomparably greater influence than upon the neurotic. Thus it can forgo even the knowledge of the individual childhood experiences of the various members of the group under investigation; from the knowledge of the socially conditioned life pattern in which these people were situated after the early years of childhood, it can acquire an understanding of the psychic attitudes common to them.

The posing of the problem of social-psychological investigation corresponds to its methodology. It wishes to investigate how certain psychic attitudes common to members of a group are related to their common life experiences. It is no more an accident in the case of an individual whether this or that libido direction dominates, whether the Oedipus complex finds this or that outlet, than it is an accident if changes in psychic characteristics occur in the psychic situation of a group, either in the same class of people over a period of time or simultaneously among different classes. It is the task of social psychology to indicate why such changes occur and how they are to be understood on the basis of the experience common to the members of the group.

The present investigation is concerned with a narrowly limited problem of social psychology, namely, the question concerning the motives conditioning the evolution of concepts about the relation of God the Father to Jesus from the beginning of Christianity to the formulation of the Nicene Creed in the fourth century. In accordance with the theoretical principles just set forth, this investigation aims to determine the extent to which the change in certain religious ideas is an expression of the psychic change of the people involved and the extent to which these changes are conditioned by their conditions of life. It will attempt to understand the ideas in terms of men and their life patterns, and to show that the evolution of dogma can be understood only through knowledge of the unconscious upon which external reality works and which determines the content of consciousness.

The method of this work necessitates that relatively large space be devoted to the presentation of the life situation of the people investigated, to their spiritual, economic, social, and political situation—in short, to their "psychic surfaces". If this seems to involve a disproportionate emphasis, the reader should bear in mind that even in the psychoanalytic case study of an ill person, great space is given to the presentation of the external circumstances surrounding the person. In the present work the description of the total cultural situation of the masses of people being investigated and the presentation of their external environment are more decisive than the description of the actual situation in a case study. The reason for this is that in the nature of things the historical reconstruction, even though it is supposed to be offered only to a certain extent in detail and plastically, is incomparably more complicated and more extensive than the report of simple facts as they occur in the life of an individual. We believe, however, that this disadvantage must be tolerated, because only in this way can an analytical understanding of historical phenomena be achieved.

The present study is concerned with a subject that has been treated by one of the most prominent representatives of the analytic study of religion, Theodor Reik.[4] The difference in content, which necessarily results from the different methodology, will, like the methodological differences themselves, be considered briefly at the end of this essay.

Our purpose here is to understand the change in certain contents of consciousness as expressed in theological ideas as the result of a change in unconscious processes. Accordingly, just as we have done with regard to the methodological problem, we propose to deal briefly with the most important findings of psychoanalysis as they touch upon our question.

2. THE SOCIAL-PSYCHOLOGICAL FUNCTION OF RELIGION

Psychoanalysis is a psychology of drives or impulses. It sees human behaviour as conditioned and defined by emotional drives, which it interprets as an outflow of certain physiologically

[4] *Dogma und Zwangsidee*, Imago, XII, 1927. Cf. *Dogma and Compulsion*, International Universities Press, 1951, and other work on psychology of religion by Reik; E. Jones, *Zur Psychoanalyse der christlichen Religion*; and A. J. Storfer, *Marias jungfräuliche Mutterschaft*, Berlin, 1913.

rooted impulses themselves not subject to immediate observation. Consistent with the popular classifications of hunger drives and love drives, from the beginning Freud distinguished between the ego or self-preservation drives, and the sexual drives. Because of the libidinous character of the ego drives of self-preservation and because of the special significance of destructive tendencies in the psychic apparatus of man, Freud suggested a different grouping, taking into account a contrast between life-maintaining and destructive drives. This classification needs no further discussion here. What is important is the recognition of certain qualities of the sex drives that distinguish them from the ego drives. The sex drives are not imperative; that is, it is possible to leave their demands ungratified without menacing life itself, which would not be the case with continued failure to satisfy hunger, thirst, and the need for sleep. Furthermore, the sex drives, up to a certain and not insignificant point, permit a gratification in fantasies and with one's own body; they are therefore much more independent of external reality than are the ego drives. Closely connected with this are the easy transference and capacity for interchange among the component impulses of sexuality. The frustration of a libidinal impulse can be relatively easily offset by the substitution of another impulse that can be gratified. This flexibility and versatility within the sexual drives are the basis for the extraordinary variability of the psychic structure and therein lies also the basis for the possibility that individual experiences can so definitely and markedly affect the libido structure. Freud sees the pleasure principle modified by the reality principle as the regulator of the psychic apparatus. He says:

> We will therefore turn to the less ambitious question of what men themselves show by their behaviour to be the purpose and intention of their lives. What do they demand of life and wish to achieve in it? The answer to this can hardly be in doubt. They

> strive after happiness; they want to become happy and remain so. This endeavour has two sides, a positive and a negative aim. It aims, on the one hand, at an absence of pain and unpleasure, and, on the other, at the experiencing of strong feelings of pleasure. In its narrower sense the word "happiness" only relates to the last. In conformity with this dichotomy in his aims, man's activity develops in two directions, according as it seeks to realize—in the main, or even exclusively—the one or the other of these aims.[5]

The individual strives to experience—under given circumstances—a maximum of libido gratification and a minimum of pain; in order to avoid pain, changes or even frustrations of the different component sex impulses can be accepted. A corresponding renunciation of the ego impulses, however, is impossible.

The peculiarity of an individual's emotional structure depends upon his psychic constitution and primarily upon his experiences in infancy. External reality, which guarantees him the satisfaction of certain impulses, but which compels the renunciation of certain others, is defined by the existing social situation in which he lives. This social reality includes the wider reality which embraces all members of society and the narrow reality of distinct social classes.

Society has a double function for the psychic situation of the individual, both frustrating and satisfying. A person seldom renounces impulses because he sees the danger resulting from their satisfaction. Generally, society dictates such renunciations: first, those prohibitions established on the basis of social recognition of a real danger *for the individual himself*, a danger not readily sensed by him and connected with the gratification of impulse; second, repression and frustration of impulses whose satisfaction

[5] *Civilization and Its Discontents* (Standard edition, XXI), p. 76.

would involve harm not to the individual but to the group; and, finally, renunciations made not in the interest of the group but only in the interest of a controlling class.

The "gratifying" function of society is no less clear than its frustrating role. The individual accepts it only because through its help he can to a certain degree count on gaining pleasure and avoiding pain, primarily with regard to the satisfaction of the elementary needs of self-preservation and, secondarily, in relation to the satisfaction of libidinous needs.

What has been said has not taken into account a specific feature of all historically known societies. The members of a society do not indeed consult one another to determine what the society can permit and what it must prohibit. Rather, the situation is that so long as the productive forces of the economy do not suffice to afford to all an adequate satisfaction of their material and cultural needs (that is, beyond protection against external danger and the satisfaction of elementary ego needs), the most powerful social class will aspire to the maximum satisfaction of their own needs first. The degree of satisfaction they provide for those who are ruled by them depends on the level of economic possibilities available, and also on the fact that a minimum satisfaction must be granted to those who are ruled so that they may be able to continue to function as co-operating members of the society. Social stability depends relatively little upon the use of external force. It depends for the most part upon the fact that men find themselves in a psychic condition that roots them inwardly in an existing social situation. For that purpose, as we have noted, a minimum of satisfaction of the natural and cultural instinctual needs is necessary. But at this point we must observe that for the psychic submission of the masses, something else is important, something connected with the peculiar structural stratification of the society into classes.

In this connexion Freud has pointed out that man's helplessness in the face of nature is a repetition of the situation in which the adult found himself as a child, when he could not do without help against unfamiliar superior forces, and when his life impulses, following their narcissistic inclinations, attached themselves first to the objects that afforded him protection and satisfaction, namely, his mother and his father. To the extent that society is helpless with respect to nature, the psychic situation of childhood must be repeated for the individual member of the society as an adult. He transfers from father or mother some of his childish love and fear and also some of his hostility to a fantasy figure, to God.

In addition, there is a hostility to certain real figures, in particular to representatives of the ruling classes. In the social stratification, the infantile situation is repeated for the individual. He sees in the rulers the powerful ones, the strong, and the wise—persons to be revered. He believes that they wish him well; he also knows that resistance to them is always punished; he is content when by docility he can win their praise. These are the identical feelings which, as a child, he had for his father, and it is understandable that he is as disposed to believe uncritically what is presented to him by the rulers as just and true, as in childhood he used to believe without criticism every statement made by his father. The figure of God forms a supplement to this situation; God is always the ally of the rulers. When the latter, who are always real personalities, are exposed to criticism, they can rely on God, who, by virtue of his unreality, only scorns criticism and, by his authority, confirms the authority of the ruling class.

In this psychological situation of the infantile bondage of the ruled to the rulers, resides one of the principal guarantees of social stability. The ruled are willing to forgo the satisfaction of certain instinctual impulses in favour of the rulers; they are willing to respect the latter's threats of punishment and to believe in the wisdom of their injunctions. They find themselves in the same situation as that in which, as helpless children, they stood in relation to the father, because the same mechanisms operate now as operated in childhood. This psychic situation becomes established through a great many significant and complicated measures taken by the ruling class, whose function it is to maintain and strengthen in the masses their infantile psychic dependence and to impose itself on their unconscious as a father figure.

One of the principal means of achieving this purpose is religion. It has the task of preventing any psychic independence on the part of the masses, of intimidating them intellectually, of bringing them into the socially necessary infantile docility toward the rulers. At the same time it has another essential function: it offers the masses a certain measure of satisfaction that makes life sufficiently tolerable for them to prevent them from attempting to change their position from that of obedient son to that of rebellious son.

Of what sort are these satisfactions? Certainly not satisfactions of the ego drives of self-preservation, nor better food nor other material pleasures. Such pleasures are to be obtained only in reality, and for that purpose one needs no religion; religion serves merely to make it easier for the masses to resign themselves to the many frustrations that reality presents. The satisfactions religion offers are of a libidinous nature; they are satisfactions that occur essentially in fantasy because, as we have pointed out before, libidinous impulses, in contrast to ego impulses, permit satisfaction in fantasies.

Here we confront a question concerning one of the psychic functions of religion, and we shall now indicate briefly the most important results of Freud's investigations in this area. In *Totem and Taboo*, Freud has shown that the animal god of totemism is the elevated father; that in the prohibition to kill and eat the totem animal and in the contrary festive custom of nevertheless violating the prohibition once a year, man repeats the ambivalent attitude which he had acquired as a child toward the father who is simultaneously a helping protector and an oppressive rival.

It has been shown, especially by Reik, that this transfer to God of the infantile attitude toward the father is found also in the great religions. The emotional attitude of the believing Christian or Jew toward his God reveals the same ambivalent characteristics as that of the child toward his father. The question posed by Freud and his students concerned the psychic quality of the religious attitude toward God; and the answer is that in the adult's attitude toward God, one sees repeated the infantile attitude of the child toward his father. This infantile psychic situation represents the pattern of the religious situation. In his *Future of an Illusion*, Freud passes beyond this question to a broader one. He no longer asks only how religion is psychologically possible; he asks also why religion exists at all or why it has been necessary. To this question he gives an answer that takes into consideration psychic and social facts simultaneously. He attributes to religion the effect of a narcotic capable of bringing some consolation to man in his impotence and helplessness before the forces of nature:

> For this situation is nothing new. It has an infantile prototype, of which it is in fact only the continuation. For once before one has found oneself in a similar state of helplessness: as a small child, in relation to one's parents. One had reason to fear them, and especially one's father; and yet one was sure of his protection against the dangers one knew. Thus it was natural to assimilate the two situations. Here, too, wishing played its part, as it does in dream-life. The sleeper may be seized with a presentiment of death, which threatens to place him in the grave. But the dream-work knows how to select a condition that will turn even that dreaded event into a wish-fulfilment: the dreamer sees himself in an ancient Etruscan grave which he has climbed down into, happy to find his archaeological interests satisfied. In the same way, a man makes the forces of nature not simply into persons with whom he can associate as he would with his equals—that would not do justice to the

> overpowering impression which those forces make on him—but he gives them the character of a father. He turns them into gods, following in this, as I have tried to show, not only an infantile prototype but a phylogenetic one.
>
> In the course of time the first observations were made of regularity and conformity to law in natural phenomena, and with this the forces of nature lost their human traits. But man's helplessness remains and along with it his longing for his father, and the gods. The gods retain their threefold task: they must exorcize the terrors of nature, they must reconcile men to the cruelty of Fate, particularly as it is shown in death, and they must compensate them for the sufferings and privations which a civilized life in common has imposed on them.[6]

Freud thus answers the question, "What constitutes the inner power of religious doctrines and to what circumstances do these doctrines owe their effectiveness independently of rational approval?"

> These [religious ideas], which are given out as teachings, are not precipitates of experience or end-results of thinking: they are illusions, fulfilments of the oldest, strongest and most urgent wishes of mankind. The secret of their strength lies in the strength of those wishes. As we already know, the terrifying impression of helplessness in childhood aroused the need for protection—for protection through love—which was provided by the father; and the recognition that this helplessness lasts throughout life made it necessary to cling to the existence of a father, but this time a more powerful one. Thus the benevolent rule of a divine Providence allays our fear of the dangers of life; the establishment of a moral world-order ensures the fulfilment of the demands of justice, which have so often remained

[6] *The Future of an Illusion* (Standard edition, XXI), pp. 17–18.

> unfulfilled in human civilization; and the prolongation of earthly existence in a future life provides the local and temporal framework in which these wish-fulfilments shall take place. Answers to the riddles that tempt the curiosity of man, such as how the universe began or what the relation is between body and mind, are developed in conformity with the underlying assumptions of this system. It is an enormous relief to the individual psyche if the conflicts of its childhood arising from the father-complex—conflicts which it has never wholly overcome—are removed from it and brought to a solution which is universally accepted.[7]

Freud therefore sees the possibility of the religious attitude in the infantile situation; he sees its relative necessity in man's impotence and helplessness with respect to nature, and he draws the conclusion that with man's increasing control over nature, religion is to be viewed as an illusion that is becoming superfluous.

Let us summarize what has been said thus far. Man strives for a maximum of pleasure; social reality compels him to many renunciations of impulse, and society seeks to compensate the individual for these renunciations by other satisfactions harmless for the society—that is, for the ruling class.

These satisfactions are such as in essence can be realized in fantasies, especially in collective fantasies. They perform an important function in social reality. In so far as society does not permit real satisfactions, fantasy satisfactions serve as a substitute and become a powerful support of social stability. The greater the renunciations men endure in reality, the stronger must be the concern for compensation. Fantasy satisfactions have the double function which is characteristic of every narcotic: they act both as an anodyne and as a deterrent to active change of

[7] Ibid, p. 30.

reality. The common fantasy satisfactions have an essential advantage over individual daydreams: by virtue of their universality, the fantasies are perceived by the conscious mind as if they were real. An illusion shared by everyone becomes a reality. The oldest of these collective fantasy satisfactions is religion. With the progressive development of society, fantasies become more complicated and more rationalized. Religion itself becomes more differentiated, and beside it appear poetry, art, and philosophy as the expressions of collective fantasies.

To sum up, religion has a threefold function: for all mankind, consolation for the privations exacted by life; for the great majority of men, encouragement to accept emotionally their class situation; and for the ruling classes, relief from guilt feelings caused by the suffering of those whom they oppress.

The following investigation aims to test in detail what has been said by examining a small segment of religious development. We shall attempt to show what influence social reality had in a specific situation upon a specific group of men, and how emotional trends found expression in certain dogmas, in collective fantasies; and to show further what psychic change was brought about by a change in the social situation. We shall try to see how this psychic change found expression in new religious fantasies that satisfied certain unconscious impulses. It will thereby become clear how closely a change in religious concepts is connected, on the one hand, with the experiencing of various possible infantile relationships to the father or mother, and on the other hand, with the change of attitude toward the ruling class and its representatives, that is, with changes in the social and economic situation.

The course of the investigation is determined by the methodological presuppositions mentioned earlier. The aim will be *to understand dogma on the basis of a study of people, not people on the basis of dogma*. We shall attempt, therefore, first to describe the total situation of the social class from which the early Christian faith originated, and to understand the psychological meaning of this faith in terms of the total psychic situation of these people. We shall then show how different the mentality of the people was at a later period; eventually, we shall try to understand the unconscious meaning of the Christology which crystallized as the end product of a three-hundred-year development. We shall treat mainly the primitive Christian faith and the Nicene dogma.

3. EARLY CHRISTIANITY AND ITS IDEA OF JESUS

Every attempt to understand the origin of Christianity must begin with an investigation of the economic, social, cultural, and psychic situation of its earliest believers.[8]

Palestine was a part of the Roman Empire and succumbed to the conditions of its economic and social development. The Augustan principate had meant the end of domination by a feudal oligarchy, and helped bring about the triumph of urban citizenry. Increasing international commerce meant no improvement for the great masses, no greater satisfaction for their everyday needs; only the thin stratum of the owning class was interested in it. An unemployed and hungry proletariat of unprecedented size filled the cities. Next to Rome, Jerusalem was the city with relatively the largest proletariat of this kind. The artisans, who usually worked only at home and belonged largely to the proletariat, easily made common cause with beggars, unskilled workers, and peasants. Indeed, the Jerusalem proletariat was in a worse situation than the Roman. It did not enjoy Roman civil rights, nor were its urgent needs of stomach and

[8] For the economic development, see especially M. Rostovtzeff, *Social and Economic History of the Roman Empire*, Oxford, 1926; Max Weber, "Die sozialen Gründe des Untergangs der antiken Kultur", in *Gesammelte Aufsätze zur Sozial- und Wirtschaftsgeschichte*, 1924; E. Meyer, "Sklaverei im Altertum", *Kleine Schriften*, 2d ed., Vol. I; K. Kautsky, *Foundations of Christianity*, Russell, 1953.

heart provided for by the emperors through great distributions of grain and elaborate games and spectacles.

The rural population was exhausted by an extraordinarily heavy tax burden, and either fell into debt slavery, or, among the small farmers, the means of production or the small landholdings were all taken away. Some of these farmers swelled the ranks of the large-city proletariat of Jerusalem; others resorted to desperate remedies, such as violent political uprising and plundering. Above this improverished and despairing proletariat, there arose in Jerusalem, as throughout the Roman Empire, a middle economic class which, though suffering under Roman pressure, was nevertheless economically stable. Above this group was the small but powerful and influential class of the feudal, priestly, and moneyed aristocracy. Corresponding to the severe economic cleavage within the Palestinian population, there was social differentiation. Pharisees, Sadducees, and Zealots were the political and religious groups representing these differences. The Sadducees represented the rich upper class: "[their] doctrine is received but by a few, yet by those of the greatest dignity."[9] Josephus refers to their aristocratic manners in another passage: "The behaviour of the Sadducees one toward another is in some degree wild; and then conversation with those that are of their own party is as barbarous as if they were strangers to them."[10]

Alongside this small feudal upper class were the Pharisees, representing the middle and smaller urban citizenry, "who are friendly to one another, and are for the exercise of concord and regard for the public".[11]

[9] The *Works of Flavius Josephus*, XVIII, 1 4, translated by William Whiston (Philadelphia, 1896).

[10] *History of the Jewish Wars*, II, 8, 14.

[11] Ibid., II, 8, 14.

> Now, for the Pharisees, they live meanly, and despise delicacies in diet; and they follow the conduct of reason, and what that prescribes to them as good for them, they do; and they think they ought earnestly to strive to observe reason's dictates for practice. They also pay respect to such as are in years; nor are they so bold as to contradict them in anything they have introduced; and, when they determine that all things are done by fate, they do not take away from men the freedom of acting as they think fit; since their notion is, that it hath pleased God that events should be decided in part by the counsel of fate, in part by such men as will accede thereunto acting therein virtuously or viciously. They also believe that souls have an immortal vigour in them, and that under the earth there will be rewards or punishments, according as they have lived virtuously or viciously in this life; and the latter are to be detained in an everlasting prison, but that the former shall have power to revive and live again; on account of which doctrines, they are able greatly to persuade the body of the people, and whatsoever they do about divine worship, prayers, and sacrifices, they perform them according to their direction.[12]

Josephus' description of the middle class of the Pharisees is doubtless more unified than it was in reality. Among the following of the Pharisees were elements that stemmed from the lowest proletarian strata that continued their relationship with them in their way of life (for example, Rabbi Akiba). At the same time, however, there were members of the well-to-do urban citizenry. This social difference found expression in different ways, most clearly in the political contradictions within Pharisaism, according as they were aroused over the question of Roman rule and revolutionary movements. But despite this differentiation, the Pharisees at first constituted a comparatively unified middle-class

[12] *Jewish Antiquities*, XVIII, 1, 3.

group under the leadership of an intellectual class that ruled the people spiritually and represented authority for the masses.

The lowest stratum of the urban *Lumpenproletariat* and of the oppressed peasants, the so-called "*Am-Haarez*" (literally, land folk), stood in sharp opposition to the Pharisees and their wider following. In fact, they were a class that had been completely uprooted by the economic development: they had nothing to lose and perhaps something to gain. They stood economically and socially outside the Jewish society integrated into the whole of the Roman Empire. They did not follow the Pharisees and did not revere them; they hated them and in turn were despised by them. Entirely characteristic of this attitude is the statement of Akiba, one of the most important Pharisees, who himself stemmed from the proletariat: "When I was still a common [ignorant] man of the Am-Haarez, I used to say: 'If I could lay my hands on a scholar I would bite him like an ass.' "[13] The Talmud goes on: "Rabbi, say 'like a dog', an ass does not bite," and he replied: "When an ass bites he generally breaks the bones of his victim, while a dog bites only the flesh." We find in the same passage in the Talmud a series of statements describing the relations between the Pharisees and the Am-Haarez.

> A man should sell all his possessions and secure the daughter of a scholar for a wife, and if he cannot secure the daughter of a scholar, he should try to obtain a daughter of a prominent man. If he cannot succeed in that, he should endeavour to obtain a daughter of a synagogue director, and if he cannot succeed in that, he should try to obtain a daughter of an alms collector, and if he cannot succeed even in this, he should try and obtain the daughter of an elementary-school teacher. He should avoid wedding the daughter of a common person [a member of the Am-Haarez], for she is an abomination, their women are

[13] Talmud, Pesachim 49b.

> an abhorrence, and concerning their daughters it is said, "Accursed be any who sleepeth with a cow" (*Deut.* 27).

Or, again, R. Jochanan says:

> One may tear a common person to pieces like a fish. . . . One who gives his daughter to a common person in marriage virtually shackles her before a lion, for just as a lion tears and devours his victim without shame, so does a common person who sleeps brutally and shamelessly with her.

R. Eliezer says:

> If the common people did not need us for economic reasons, they would long ago have slain us. . . . The enmity of a common person toward a scholar is even more intense than that of the heathens towards the Israelites . . . Six things are true of the common person: One may depend upon no common person as a witness and may accept no evidence from him, one may not let him share a secret, nor be a ward for an orphan, nor a trustee of funds for charitable funds, one may not go on a journey in his company and one should not tell him if he has lost something.[14]

The views here cited (which could be multiplied considerably) stem from Pharisaic circles and show with what hatred they opposed the Am-Haarez, but also with what bitterness the common man may have hated the scholars and their following.[15]

[14] All of the passages cited above are in the Talmud, Pesachim 49b.
[15] Cf. Friedlander, *Die religiösen Bewegungen innerhalb des Judentums im Zeitalter Jesu*, Berlin, 1905.

It has been necessary to describe the opposition within Palestinian Judaism between the aristocracy, the middle classes and their intellectual leaders on the one hand, and the urban and rural proletariat on the other, in order to make clear the underlying causes of such political and religious revolutionary movements as early Christianity. A more extensive presentation of the differentiation among the extraordinarily variegated Pharisees is not necessary for the purpose of the present study and would lead us too far afield. The oppositions between the bourgeoisie and the proletariat within the Pharisaic group increased, as Roman oppression became heavier and the lowest classes more economically crushed and uprooted. To the same extent the lowest classes of society became the supporters of the national, social, and religious revolutionary movements.

These revolutionary aspirations of the masses found expression in two directions: political attempts at revolt and emancipation directed against their own aristocracy and the Romans, and in all sorts of religious-messianic movements. But there is by no means a sharp separation between these two streams moving toward liberation and salvation; often they flow into each other. The messianic movements themselves assumed partly practical and partly merely literary forms.

The most important movements of this sort may be briefly mentioned here.

Shortly before Herod's death, that is, at a time when, in addition to Roman domination, the people suffered oppression at the hands of Jewish deputies serving under the Romans, there took place in Jerusalem, under the leadership of two Pharisaic scholars, a popular revolt, during which the Roman eagle at the entrance to the Temple was destroyed. The instigators were executed, and the chief plotters were burned alive. After Herod's death a mob demonstrated before his successor, Archelaus, demanding the release of the political prisoners, the abolition of the market tax, and a reduction in the annual tribute. These demands were not satisfied. A great popular demonstration in connexion with these events in the year 4 B.C. was suppressed with bloodshed, thousands of demonstrators being killed by the soldiers. Nevertheless, the movement became stronger. Popular revolt progressed. Seven weeks later in Jerusalem it mounted to new bloody revolts against Rome. In addition, the rural population was roused. In the old revolutionary centre, Galilee, there were many struggles with the Romans, and in Transjordan there was rioting. A former shepherd assembled voluntary troops and led a guerrilla war against the Romans.

This was the situation in the year 4 B.C. The Romans did not find it altogether easy to cope with the revolting masses. They crowned their victory by crucifying two thousand revolutionary prisoners.

For some years the country remained quiet. But shortly after the introduction in A.D. 6 of a direct Roman administration in the country, which began its activity with a popular census for tax purposes, there was a new revolutionary movement. Now begins a separation between the lower and the middle classes. Although ten years earlier the Pharisees had joined the revolt, there developed now a new split between the urban and the rural revolutionary masses on the one side and the Pharisees on the other. The urban and rural proletariat united in a new party, namely, the Zealots, while the middle class, under the leadership of the Pharisees, was prepared for reconciliation with the Romans. The more oppressive the Roman and the aristocratic Jewish yoke became, the greater the despair of the masses, and Zealotism won new followers. Up to the outbreak of the great revolt against the Romans there were constant clashes between the people and the administration. The occasions for revolutionary outbreaks were the frequent attempts of the Romans to put up a statue of Caesar or the Roman eagle in the Temple of Jerusalem. The indignation against these measures, which were rationalized on religious grounds, stemmed in reality from the hatred of the masses for the emperor as leader and head of the ruling class oppressing them. The peculiar character of this hatred for the emperor becomes clearer if we remember that this was an epoch in which reverence for the Roman emperor was spreading widely throughout the empire and in which the emperor cult was about to become the dominant religion.

The more hopeless the struggle against Rome became on the political level, and the more the middle class withdrew and became disposed to compromise with Rome, the more radical the proletarian masses became, but the more revolutionary tendencies lost their political character and were transferred to the level of religious fantasies and messianic ideas. Thus a pseudo-messiah, Theudas, promised the masses he would lead them to the Jordan and repeat the miracle of Moses. The Jews would pass through the river with dry feet, but the pursuing Romans would drown. The Romans saw in these fantasies the expression of a dangerous revolutionary ferment; they killed the followers of this messiah and beheaded Theudas. Theudas had successors. Josephus provides an account of an uprising under the provincial governor Felix (52–60); its leaders

> deceived and deluded the people under pretence of divine inspiration, but were for procuring innovations and changes of the government; and these prevailed with the multitude to act like madmen, and went before them into the wilderness, as pretending that God would there show them the signals of liberty; but Felix thought this procedure was to be the beginning of a revolt; so he sent some horsemen, and footmen both armed, who destroyed a great number of them.
>
> But there was an Egyptian false prophet that did the Jews more mischief than the former; for he was a cheat, and pretended to be a prophet also, and got together thirty thousand men that were deluded by him: these he led round about from the wilderness to the mount which was called the Mount of

> Olives, and was ready to break into Jerusalem by force from that place.[16]

The Roman military made short shrift of the revolutionary hordes. Most of them were killed or put in prison, the rest destroyed themselves; all tried to remain in hiding at home. Nevertheless, the uprisings continued:

> Now, when these were quieted, it happened, as it does in a diseased body, that another part was subject to an inflammation; for a company of deceivers and robbers [that is, the messianists and more politically-minded revolutionaries] got together, and persuaded the Jews to revolt, and exhorted them to assert their liberty, inflicting death on those that continued in obedience to the Roman government, and saying, that such as willingly chose slavery, ought to be forced from such their desired inclinations [that is, the middle and upper classes]; for they parted themselves into different bodies, and lay in wait up and down the country, and plundered the houses of the great men, and slew the men themselves, and set the villages on fire; and this till all Judea was filled with the effects of their madness. And thus the flame was every day more and more blown up, till it came to a direct war.[17]

The growing oppression of the lower classes of the nation brought about a sharpening of the conflict between them and the less oppressed middle class, and in this process the masses became more and more radical. The left wing of the Zealots formed a secret faction of the "Sicarii" (dagger carriers), who began through attacks and plots to exert a terroristic pressure on

[16] *History of the Jewish Wars*, II, 13, 4, 5.

[17] Ibid., II, 13, 6. It is important to note that Josephus, who himself belonged to the aristocratic *élite*, is describing the revolutionaries in terms of his own bias.

the well-to-do citizens. Without mercy they persecuted the moderates and the appeasers in the higher and middle classes of Jerusalem; at the same time they invaded, plundered, and reduced to ashes the villages whose inhabitants refused to join their revolutionary bands. The prophets and the pseudo-messiahs likewise did not cease their agitation among the common folk.

Finally, in the year 66 the great popular revolt against Rome broke out. It was supported first by the middle and lower classes of the nation, who in severe struggles overcame the Roman troops. At first the war was led by the property owners and the educated, but they acted with little energy and with the tendency to arrive at a compromise. The first year, therefore, ended in failure despite several victories, and the masses attributed the unhappy outcome to the weak and indifferent early direction of the war. The leaders of the masses attempted by every means to seize power and to put themselves in the place of the existing leaders. Since the latter did not leave their positions voluntarily, there came in the winter of 67–68 "a bloody civil war and abominable scenes, such as only the French Revolution may boast".[18] The more hopeless the war became, the more the middle classes tried their luck in a compromise with the Romans; as a result, the civil war grew more fierce, together with the struggle against the foreign enemy.[19]

While Rabbi Jochanan ben Sakkai, one of the leading Pharisees, went over to the enemy and made peace with him, the small tradesmen, artisans, and peasants defended the city against the Romans with great heroism for five months. They had nothing to lose but also nothing more to gain, for the struggle against the Roman power was hopeless and had to end in collapse. Many of

[18] E. Schürer, *Geschichte des jüdischen Volkes im Zeitalter Jesu Christi*, 3rd ed., 1901, Vol. I, 617.

[19] Cf. T. Mommsen, *History of Rome*, Vol. V.

the well-to-do were able to save themselves by going over to the Romans, and although Titus was extremely embittered against the remaining Jews he nevertheless admitted those who were in flight. At the same time the embattled masses of Jerusalem stormed the King's palace into which many of the well-to-do Jews had brought their treasures, took the money, and killed the owners. The Roman war and the civil war ended with victory for the Romans. This was accompanied by the victory of the ruling Jewish group and the collapse of a hundred thousand Jewish peasants and the urban lower classes.[20]

Alongside the political and social struggles and the messianically coloured revolutionary attempts are the popular writings originating at that time and inspired by the same tendencies: namely, the apocalyptic literature. Despite its variety, the vision of the future in this apocalyptic literature is comparatively uniform. First there are the "Woes of the Messiah" (*Macc.* 13:7, 8), which refer to events that will not trouble "the elect"—famine, earthquakes, epidemics, and wars. Then comes the "great affliction" prophesied in *Daniel* 12:1, such as has not occurred since the creation of the world, a frightening time of suffering and distress. Throughout apocalyptic literature in general there runs the belief that the elect will also be protected from this affliction. The horror of desolation prophesied in *Daniel* 9:27, 11:31, and 12:11 represents the final sign of the end. The picture of the end bears old prophetic features. The climax will be the appearance of the Son of Man on the clouds in great splendour and glory.[21]

Just as in the struggle against the Romans, the different classes of people participated in different ways, so apocalyptic literature, too, originated in different classes. Despite a certain uniformity, this is clearly expressed by the difference in emphasis on individual elements within the various apocalyptic writings. Despite

[20] Josephus, *History of the Roman War*, Vol. VI.

[21] Cf. Johannes Weiss, *Das Urchristentum*, Göttingen, 1917.

the impossibility of detailed analysis here, we may cite as an expression of the same revolutionary tendencies that inspired the left wing of the defenders of Jerusalem, the concluding exhortation of the Book of Enoch:

> Woe to those that build their homes with sand; for they will be overthrown from their foundation and will fall by the sword. But those who acquire gold and silver will perish in the judgment suddenly. Woe to you ye rich, for ye have trusted in your riches and from your riches ye shall be torn away, because you have not remembered the most High in the days of judgment. . . . Woe to you who requite your neighbour with evil, for you will be requited according to your works. Woe to you lying witnesses. . . . Fear not, ye that suffer, for healing will be your portion: A bright light will shine and you will hear the voice of rest from heaven (*Enoch* 94–96).

Besides these religious-messianic, socio-political, and literary movements characteristic of the time of the rise of Christianity, another movement must be mentioned in which political goals played no role and which led directly to Christianity, namely, the movement of John the Baptist. He enkindled a popular movement. The upper class, regardless of its persuasion, would have nothing to do with him. His most attentive listeners came from the ranks of the despised masses.[22] He preached that the kingdom of heaven and judgment day were at hand, bringing deliverance for the good, destruction for the evil. "Repent ye, for the kingdom of heaven is at hand" was the burden of his preaching.

To understand the psychological meaning of the first Christians' faith in Christ—and this is the primary purpose of

[22] Cf. M. Dibelius, *Die urchristliche Ueberlieferung von Johannes dem Taufer*, Stuttgart, 1911.

the present study—it is necessary for us to visualize what kind of people supported early Christianity. They were the masses of the uneducated poor, the proletariat of Jerusalem, and the peasants in the country who, because of the increasing political and economic oppression and because of social restriction and contempt, increasingly felt the urge to change existing conditions. They longed for a happy time for themselves, and also harboured hate and revenge against both their own rulers and the Romans. We have observed how varied were the forms of these tendencies, ranging from the political struggle against Rome to the class struggle in Jerusalem, from Theudas' unrealistic revolutionary attempts to John the Baptist's movement and the apocalyptic literature. From political activity to messianic dreams were all sorts of different phenomena; yet behind all these different forms was the same motivating force: the hatred and the hope of the suffering masses, caused by their distress and the inescapability of their socio-economic situation. Whether the eschatological expectation had more social, more political, or more religious content, it became stronger with the increasing oppression, and more active "the deeper we descend into the illiterate masses, to the so-called Am-Haarez, the circle of those who experienced the present as oppression and therefore had to look to the future for the fulfilment of all their wishes".[23]

The bleaker the hope for real improvement became, the more this hope had to find expression in fantasies. The Zealots' desperate final struggle against the Romans and John the Baptist's movement were the two extremes, and were rooted in the same soil: the despair of the lowest classes. This stratum is psychologically characterized by the presence of hope for a change in their condition (analytically interpreted, for a good father who would help them), and, at the same time, a fierce hatred of oppressors, which found expression in feelings directed against

[23] Ibid., p. 130.

the Roman emperor, the Pharisees, the rich in general, and in the fantasies of punishment of the Day of Judgment. We see here an ambivalent attitude: these people loved in fantasy a good father who would help and deliver them, and they hated the evil father who oppressed, tormented, and despised them.

From this stratum of the poor, uneducated, revolutionary masses Christianity arose as a significant historical messianic-revolutionary movement. Like John the Baptist, early Christian doctrine addressed itself not to the educated and the property owners, but to the poor, the oppressed, and the suffering. The small artisans and the proletarians supported the new message.[24] Celsus, an opponent of the Christians, gives a good picture of the social composition of the Christian community as he saw it almost two centuries later:

He asserts:

> In private houses also we see wool-workers, cobblers, laundry-workers, and the most illiterate and bucolic yokels, who would not dare to say anything at all in front of their elders and more intelligent masters. But whenever they get hold of children in private and some stupid women with them, they let out some astounding statements as, for example, that they must not pay any attention to their father and school-teachers, but must obey them; they say that these talk nonsense and have no understanding, and that in reality they neither know nor are able to do anything good, but are taken up with mere empty chatter. But they alone, they say, know the right way to live, and if the

[24] Cf. for the social structure of primitive Christianity, R. Knopf, *Das nachapostolische Zeitalter*, Tübingen, 1905; Adolf Harnack, *Die Mission und Ausbreitung des Christentums*, 4th ed., 1923, Vol. 1; Adolf Harnack, "Kirche und Staat bis zur Gründung der Staatskirche", *Kultur der Gegenwart*, 2nd ed.; Adolf Harnack, "Des Urchristentum und die soziale Frage", *Preussische Jahrbücher*, 1908, Vol. 131; K. Kautsky, *Foundations of Christianity*, Russell, 1953.

> children would believe them, they would become happy and make their home happy as well. And if just as they are speaking they see one of the school-teachers coming, or some intelligent person, or even the father himself, the more cautions of them flee in all directions; but the more reckless urge the children on to rebel. They whisper to them that in the presence of their father and their schoolmasters they do not feel able to explain anything to the children, since they do not want to have anything to do with the silly and obtuse teachers who are totally corrupted and far gone in wickedness and who inflict punishment on the children. But, if they like, they should leave father and their schoolmasters, and go along with the women and little children who are their play-fellows to the wooldresser's shop, or to the cobbler's or the washerwoman's shop, that they may learn perfection. And by saying this they persuade them.[25]

The picture Celsus gives here of the supporters of Christianity is characteristic not only of their social but also of their psychic situation, their struggle and hatred against paternal authority.

What was the content of the primitive Christian message?[26]

In the foreground stands the eschatological expectation. Jesus preached the nearness of the kingdom of God. He taught the people to see in His activities the beginning of this new kingdom. Nevertheless,

> The completion of the kingdom will only appear when he returns in glory in the clouds of heaven to judgment. Jesus

[25] Origen, *Contra Celsum*, III, 55, translated by Henry Chadwick, Cambridge University Press, London, 1953.

[26] The problem of the historical Jesus need not concern us in this connection. Even if the primitive Christian message were the work of a single personality, its social effect is to be understood only on the basis of the classes to which it was directed and by which it was accepted; and only the understanding of their psychic situation is important for us here.

> seems to have announced this speedy return a short time before his death, and to have comforted his disciples at his departure with the assurance that he would immediately enter into a supermundane position with God.
>
> The instructions of Jesus to his disciples are accordingly dominated by the thought that the end—the day and hour of which, however, no one knows—is at hand. In consequence of this, also, the exhortation to renounce all earthly good takes a prominent place.[27]
>
> The conditions of entrance to the kingdom are, in the first place, a complete change of mind, in which a man renounces the pleasures of this world, denies himself, and is ready to surrender all that he has in order to save his soul; then, a believing trust in God's grace which he grants to the humble and the poor, and therefore hearty confidence in Jesus as the Messiah chosen and called by God to realize his kingdom on the earth. The announcement is therefore directed to the poor, the suffering, those hungering and thirsting for righteousness, not to those who live, but to those who wish to be healed and redeemed, and finds them prepared for entrance into, and reception of the blessings of the kingdom of God, while it brings down upon the self-satisfied, the rich and those proud of their righteousness, the judgment of obduracy and the damnation of Hell.[28]

The proclamation that the kingdom of heaven was at hand (Matt. 10:7) was the germ of the oldest preaching. It was this that aroused in the suffering and oppressed masses an enthusiastic hope. The feeling of the people was that everything was

[27] Harnack, Adolf: *History of Dogma*, New York, Dover Publications, 1961, I, pp. 66–7.
[28] Harnack, Adolf: *History of Dogma*, New York, Dover Publications, 1961, I, pp. 62–63.

coming to an end. They believed that there would not be time to spread Christianity among all the heathen before the new era arrived. If the hopes of the other groups of the same oppressed masses were directed to bringing about political and social revolution by their own energy and effort, the eyes of the early Christian community were focused solely on the great event, the miraculous beginning of a new age. The content of the primitive Christian message was not an economic nor a social-reform programme but the blessed promise of a not-distant future in which the poor would be rich, the hungry would be satisfied, and the oppressed would attain authority. This hope was understood in a completely literal and material sense.[29]

The mood of these first enthusiastic Christians is clearly seen in *Luke* 6:20 ff.

> Blessed are you poor, for yours is the kingdom of God.
> Blessed are you that hunger now, for you shall be satisfied.
> Blessed are you that weep now, for you shall laugh.
> Blessed are you when men hate you, and when they exclude you and revile you, and cast out your name as evil, on account of the Son of man! Rejoice in that day, and leap for joy, for behold, your reward is great in heaven; for so their fathers did to the prophets.
> But woe to you that are rich, for you have received your consolation.
> Woe to you that are full now, for you shall hunger.
> Woe to you that laugh now, for you shall mourn and weep.

These statements express not only the longing and expectation of the poor and oppressed for a new and better world, but also their complete hatred of the authorities—the rich, the

[29] Cf. Weiss, *Das Urchristentum*, p. 55.

learned, and the powerful. The same mood is found in the story of the poor man Lazarus, "who desired to be fed with what fell from the rich man's table" (*Luke* 16:21), and in the famous words of Jesus: "How hard it is for those who have riches to enter the kingdom of God! For it is easier for a camel to go through the eye of a needle than for a rich man to enter the kingdom of God" (*Luke* 18:24). The hatred of the Pharisees and the tax-collectors runs like a red thread through the Gospels, with the result that for almost two thousand years, opinion of the Pharisees throughout Christendom has been determined by this hatred.

We hear this hatred of the rich again in the Epistle of James, in the middle of the second century:

> Come now, you rich, weep and howl for the miseries that are coming upon you. Your riches have rotted and your garments are motheaten. Your gold and silver have rusted, and their rust will be evidence against you and will eat your flesh like fire. You have laid up treasure for the last days. Behold, the wages of the labourers who mowed your fields, which you kept back by fraud, cry out; and the cries of the harvesters have reached the ears of the Lord of hosts. You have lived on the earth in luxury and in pleasure; you have fattened your hearts in a day of slaughter. You have condemned, you have killed the righteous man; he does not resist you.
>
> Be patient, therefore, brethren, until the coming of the Lord . . . Behold, the Judge is standing at the doors (*James* 5:1 ff).

Speaking of this hatred, Kautsky rightly says: "Rarely has the class hatred of the modern proletariat attained such forms as that of the Christian proletariat."[30] It is the hatred of the Am-Haarez for the Pharisees, of the Zealots and the Sicarii for the well-to-do and the middle class, of the suffering and harassed people of

[30] K. Kautsky, *Der Ursprung des Christentums*, p. 345.

town and country for those in authority and in high places, as it had been expressed in the pre-Christian political rebellions and in messianic fantasies.

Intimately connected with this hatred for the spiritual and social authorities, the hatred of brothers for the father, is an essential feature of the social and psychic structure of early Christianity, namely, its democratic, brotherly character. If the Jewish society of the time was characterized by an extreme caste spirit pervading all social relationships, the early Christian community was a free brotherhood of the poor, unconcerned with institutions and formulas.

> We find ourselves confronted by an impossible task if we wish to sketch a picture of the organization during the first hundred years. . . . The whole community is held together only by the common bond of faith and hope and love. [We must add: and of hatred.] The office does not support the person, but always the person the office . . . Since the first Christians felt they were pilgrims and strangers on the earth, what need was there for permanent institutions?[31]

In this early Christian brotherhood, mutual economic assistance and support, "love-communism", as Harnack calls it, played a special role.

We see, therefore, that the early Christians were men and women, the poor, uneducated, oppressed masses of the Jewish people, and later, of other peoples. Instead of the increasing impossibility of altering their hopeless situation through realistic means, there developed the fantastic expectation that a change would occur in a very short time, at a moment's notice, and that these people would then find the happiness previously missed, but that the rich and the nobility would be punished, in

[31] H. von Schubert, *Grundzüge der Kirchengeschichte*, Tübingen, 1904.

accordance with justice and the desires of the Christian masses. The first Christians were a brotherhood of socially and economically oppressed enthusiasts held together by hope and hatred.

What distinguished the early Christians from the peasants and proletarians struggling against Rome was not their basic psychic attitude. The first Christians were no more "humble" and resigned to the will of God, no more convinced of the necessity and immutability of their lot, no more inspired by the wish to be loved by their rulers than were the political and military fighters. The two groups hated the ruling fathers in the same way, hoping with equal vigour to see the latter's downfall and the beginning of their own rule and of a satisfactory future. The difference between them lay neither in the presuppositions nor in the goal and direction of their wishes, but only in the sphere in which they tried to fulfil them. While the Zealots and Sicarii endeavoured to realize their wishes in the sphere of political reality, the complete hopelessness of realization led the early Christians to formulate the same wishes in fantasy. The expression of this wish fantasy was the early Christian faith, especially the early Christian fantasy concerning Jesus and his relationship to the Father-God.

What were the ideas of these first Christians?

> The contents of the faith of the disciples, and the common proclamation which united them, may be comprised in the following propositions. Jesus of Nazareth is the Messiah promised by the prophets. Jesus after His death is by the Divine awakening raised to the right hand of God, and will soon return to set up His kingdom visibly upon the earth. He who believes in Jesus, and has been received into the community of the disciples of Jesus, who, in virtue of a sincere change of mind, calls on God as Father, and lives according to the commandments of Jesus, is a saint of God, and as such can be certain of

> the sin-forgiving grace of God, and of a share in the future glory, that is, of redemption.[32]

"God has made him both Lord and Christ" (*Acts* 2:36). This is the oldest doctrine of Christ that we have, and is therefore of great interest, especially since it was later supplanted by other, more extensive, doctrines. It is called the "adoptionist" theory because here an act of adoption is assumed. Adoption is here used in contrast to the natural sonship which exists from birth. Accordingly, the thought present here is that Jesus was not messiah from the beginning; in other words, he was not from the beginning the Son of God, but became so only by a definite, very distinct act of God's will. This is expressed particularly in the fact that the statement in *Psalms* 2:7, "You are my son, today I have begotten you," is interpreted as referring to the moment of the exaltation of Jesus (*Acts* 13:33).

According to an ancient Semitic idea, the king is a son of God, whether by descent or, as here, by adoption, on the day he mounts the throne. It is therefore in keeping with the oriental spirit to say that Jesus, as He was exalted to the right hand of God, became the Son of God. This idea is echoed even by Paul, although for him the concept "Son of God" had already acquired another meaning. *Romans* 1:4 says of the Son of God that He was "designated Son of God in power . . . by His resurrection from the dead". Here two different forms of the concept conflict: the Son of God who was Son from the very beginning (Paul's idea); and Jesus, who, after the resurrection, was exalted to Son of God in power, that is, to kingly ruler of the world (the concept of the early community). The difficult combination of the two ideas shows very clearly that here two different thought patterns encountered each other. The older, stemming from the early Christian community, is consistent, in

[32] Harnack, *History of Dogma*, New York, 1961, 1, 78.

that the early community characterizes Jesus, before the exaltation, as a man: "a man attested to you by God with mighty works and wonders and signs which God did through Him in your midst" (*Acts* 2:22). One should observe here that Jesus has not performed the miracle, but God through Him. Jesus was the voice of God. This idea prevails to some extent in the Gospel tradition, where, for example, after the healing of the lame, the people praise God (*Mark* 2:12). In particular, Jesus is characterized as the prophet whom Moses promised: "The Lord God will raise up for you a prophet from your brethren" (*Acts* 3:22, 7:37; *Deut.* 18:15).[33]

We see thus that the concept of Jesus held by the early community was that He was a man chosen by God and elevated by Him as a "Messiah", and later as "Son of God". This Christology of the early community resembles in many respects the concept of the messiah chosen by God to introduce a kingdom of righteousness and love, a concept which had been familiar among the Jewish masses for a long time. In only two ideas of the new faith do we find elements that signify something specifically new: in the fact of His exaltation as Son of God to sit at the right hand of the Almighty, and in the fact that this messiah is no longer the powerful, victorious hero, but His significance and dignity reside just in His suffering, in His death on the cross. To be sure, the idea of a dying messiah or even of a dying god was not entirely new in the popular consciousness. *Isaiah* 53 speaks of this suffering servant of God. The Fourth Book of Ezra also mentions a dying messiah, although of course in an essentially different form, for he dies after four hundred years and after his victory.[34] The idea of a dying god may have become familiar to the people from

[33] J. Weiss, *Das Urchristentum*, p. 85.
[34] Cf. *Psalm* 22 and *Hosea* 6.

an entirely different source, namely, the Near Eastern cults and myths (Osiris, Attis, and Adonis).

> The fate of man finds its prototype in the passion of a god who suffers on earth, dies and rises again. This god will permit all those to share in that blessed immortality who join him in the mysteries or even identify themselves with him.[35]

Perhaps there were also Jewish esoteric traditions of a dying god or a dying messiah, but all these precursors cannot explain the enormous influence which the teaching about the crucified and suffering saviour immediately had upon the Jewish masses and soon upon the pagan masses as well.

In the early community of enthusiasts, Jesus was thus a man exalted after His death into a God who would soon return in order to execute judgment, to make happy those who suffer, and to punish the rulers.

We have now gained insight into the psychic surfaces of the followers of early Christianity sufficiently to attempt our interpretation of these first Christological fantasies. Those intoxicated by this idea were people who were tormented and despairing, full of hatred for their Jewish and pagan oppressors, with no prospect of effecting a better future. A message which would allow them to project into fantasy all that reality had denied them must have been extremely fascinating.

If there was nothing left for the Zealots but to die in hopeless battle, the followers of Christ could dream of their goal without reality immediately showing them the hopelessness of their wishes. By substituting fantasy for reality, the Christian message satisfied the longings for hope and revenge, and although it

[35] F. Cumont, "Die orientalischen Religionen in ihrem Einfluss auf die europäischen Religionen des Altertums", *Kultur der Gegenwart*, 2nd ed., 1923, Vol. I, III, 1; cf. also Weiss, op. cit. p. 70.

failed to relieve hunger, it brought a fantasy satisfaction of no little significance for the oppressed.[36]

Our psychoanalytic investigation of the Christological faith of the early Christian community must now raise the following questions: What was the significance for the first Christians of the fantasy of the dying man elevated to a god? Why did this fantasy win the hearts of so many thousands in a short time? What were its unconscious sources, and what emotional needs were satisfied by it?

First, the most important question: A man is raised to a god; he is adopted by God. As Reik has correctly observed, we have

[36] A remark must be inserted here about one problem which has been the object of severe polemics, the question as to how far Christianity can be understood as a revolutionary class movement. Kautsky, in *Vorläufer des neuen Sozialismus* (Stuttgart, 1895), and later in *Foundations of Christianity*, has set forth the view that Christianity is a proletarian class movement, that in essence, however, its significance lay in its practical activity, that is, in its charitable work and not in its "pious fanaticisms". Kautsky overlooks the fact that a movement may have a class origin without the existence of social and economic motives in the consciousness of its instigation. His contempt for the historical significance of pious extravagances demonstrates only his complete lack of understanding of the meaning of fantasy satisfaction within the social process. His interpretation of historical materialism is so banal that it is easy for Troeltsch and Harnack to give an appearance of refuting historical materialism. They, following Kautsky, do not put at the centre of the inquiry the problem of the class relationship that conditioned Christianity, but rather the problem as to how much of a role these class relationships played in the consciousness and ideology of the first Christians. Since they view the problem of the social and economic programme of the first Christians as the central point of an historical-materialistic conception, they do not treat the problem of the class-conditioned character of the "pious fantasies" and their function in the class struggle, as is attempted in the present study. Although Kautsky misses the real problem, the class foundations of early Christianity are nevertheless so clear that the tortuous attempt, especially of Troeltsch (in his *Social Teaching of the Christian Churches*), to explain them away and weaken them, betrays all too plainly the political tendencies of the author.

here the old myth of the rebellion of the son, an expression of hostile impulses toward the father-god. We now understand what significance this myth must have had for the followers of early Christianity. These people hated intensely the authorities that confronted them with "fatherly" power. The priests, scholars, aristocrats, in short, all the rulers who excluded them from the enjoyment of life and who in their emotional world played the role of the severe, forbidding, threatening, tormenting father—they also had to hate this God who was an ally of their oppressors, who permitted them to suffer and be oppressed. They themselves wanted to rule, even to be the masters, but it seemed to them hopeless to try to achieve this in reality and to overthrow and destroy their present masters by force. So they satisfied their wishes in a fantasy. Consciously they did not dare to slander the fatherly God. Conscious hatred was for the ruling class only, not for the elevated father figure, the Divine Being Himself. But the unconscious hostility to the Divine Father found expression in the Christ fantasy. They put a man at God's side and made him a co-regent with God the Father. This man who became a god, and with whom as humans they could identify, represented their Oedipus wishes; he was a symbol of their unconscious hostility to God the Father, for if a man could become God, the latter was deprived of his privileged fatherly position of being unique and unreachable. The belief in the elevation of a man to God was thus the expression of unconscious wish for the removal of the Divine Father.

Here lies the significance of the fact that the early Christian community held the adoptionist doctrine, the theory of the elevation of man to God. In this doctrine the hostility to God found its expression, while in the doctrine that later increased in popularity and became dominant—the doctrine about the Jesus who was always a god—was expressed the elimination of these hostile wishes toward God (to be discussed in greater detail later). The faithful identified with this son; they could identify with

Him because He was a suffering human like themselves. This is the basis of the fascinating power and effect upon the masses of the suffering man elevated to a god: only with a suffering being could they identify. Thousands of men before Him had been crucified, tormented, and humiliated. If they thought of this crucified one as elevated to God, this meant that in their unconscious, this crucified god was themselves.

The pre-Christian apocalypse mentioned a victorious, strong messiah. He was the representative of the wishes and fantasies of a class of people who were oppressed, but who in many ways suffered less, and still harboured the hope of victory. The class from which the early Christian community grew, and in which the Christianity of the first one hundred to one hundred and fifty years had great success, could not identify with such a strong, powerful messiah; their messiah could only be a suffering, crucified one. But now another element entered in. The figure of the suffering saviour was determined in a threefold way: First in the sense just mentioned; secondly by the fact that some of the death wishes against father-god were shifted to the son. In the myth of the dying god (Adonis, Attis, Osiris), God Himself was the one whose death was fantasied. In the early Christian myth the father is killed in the son.

But, finally, the fantasy of the crucified son had still a third function: Since the believing enthusiasts were imbued with hatred and death wishes—consciously against the ruling class, unconsciously against God the Father—they identified with the crucified; they themselves suffered death on the cross and atoned in this way for their death wishes against the father. Through His death, Jesus expiated the guilt of all, and the first Christians greatly needed such an atonement. Because of their total situation, a primordial motive of the human soul (as Freud has shown in *Totem and Taboo*), aggression and death wishes against the father were particularly active in them.

The focus of the early Christian fantasy, however—in contrast to the later Catholic faith, to be dealt with presently—seems to lie, not in a masochistic expiation through self-annihilation, but in the displacement of the father by identification with the suffering Jesus.

For a full understanding of the psychic background of the belief in Christ, we must consider the fact that at that time the Roman Empire was increasingly devoted to the emperor cult, which transversed all national boundaries. Psychologically it was closely related to monotheism, the belief in a righteous, good father; and if it was propagated by the ruling classes of the Roman Empire, in their view this was quite understandable and consistent. If the pagans often referred to Christianity as atheism, in a deeper psychological sense they were right, for this faith in the suffering man elevated to a god was the fantasy of a suffering, oppressed class that wanted to displace the ruling powers—God, emperor, and father—and put themselves in their places. If the main accusations of the pagans against the Christians included the charge that they committed Oedipus crimes, this accusation was actually senseles slander; but the unconscious of the slanderers had understood well the unconscious meaning of the Christ myth, its Oedipus wishes, and its concealed hostility to God the Father, the emperor, and authority.[37]

In order to understand the later development of dogma, one must understand first the distinctive feature of early Christology, its adoptionist character. The belief that a man is elevated to a god was an expression of the unconscious impulse of hostility to the father that was present in these masses. It presented the possibility of an identification and the corresponding expectation that the new age would soon begin when those who were suffering and oppressed would be rulers and thus become happy. Since one could and did identify with Jesus because He

[37] The accusations of ritual murder and of sexual licentiousness can be understood in a similar way.

was the suffering man, the possibility was offered of a community organization without authorities, statutes, and bureaucracy, united by the common identification with the suffering Jesus raised to a god. The early Christian adoptionist belief was born of the masses; it was an expression of their revolutionary tendencies, and offered a satisfaction for their strongest longing. This explains why it so extraordinarily rapidly became the religion also of the oppressed pagan masses (although soon not theirs exclusively).

4. THE TRANSFORMATION OF CHRISTIANITY AND THE HOMOOUSIAN DOGMA

The early beliefs concerning Jesus underwent a change. The man raised to God became the Son of Man who was always God and existed before all creation, one with God and yet to be distinguished from Him. Has this change of ideas about Jesus also a socio-psychological meaning such as we were able to demonstrate for the early adoptionist belief? We shall find an answer to this question by studying the people who, two to three hundred years later, created this dogma and believed in it, to understand their real life situation and learn their psychic aspects.

The most important questions are these: Who were the Christians in the early centuries after Christ? Does Christianity remain the religion of the suffering Jewish enthusiasts of Palestine, or who takes their place and joins them?

The first great change in the composition of believers occurred when Christian propaganda turned toward the pagans, and in a great victorious campaign won followers among them in almost the entire Roman Empire. The significance of change of nationality among the followers of Christianity should not be underestimated, but it played no decisive role so long as the social composition of the Christian community did not change essentially, so long, that is, as it was made up of poor, oppressed, uneducated people feeling common suffering, common hatred, and common hope.

The familiar judgement of Paul concerning the Corinthian community holds without doubt for the second and third generations of most of the Christian communities as well as for the apostolic period:

> For consider your call, brethren; not many of you were wise according to wordly standards, not many were powerful, not many were of noble birth; but God chose what is foolish in the world to shame the wise, God chose what is weak in the world to shame the strong, God chose what is low and despised in the world, even things that are not, to bring to nothing things that are (1 *Cor.* 1:26–28).[38]

But although the great majority of the followers Paul won for Christianity in the first century were still people of the lowest classes—small artisans, slaves, and emancipated slaves—gradually another social element, the educated and the well-to-do, began to infiltrate the communities. Paul was indeed the first Christian leader that did not stem from the lower classes. He was the son of a well-to-do Roman citizen, had been a Pharisee and therefore one of the intellectuals who scorned the Christians and was hated by them.

> He was not a proletarian unfamiliar with and hatefully opposed to the political order, not one who had no interest in its continuance and who hoped for its destruction. He had from the beginning been too close to the powers of government and justice, had had too much experience of the blessings of the sacred order not to be of a quite different mind concerning the ethical worth of the state, than, say, a member of the native

[38] Knopf, *Das nachapostolische Zeitalter*, p. 64.

> Zealot party, or even than his Pharisaic colleagues who saw in the Roman domination at most the lesser evil compared with the half-Jewish Herodians.[39]

With his propaganda, Paul doubtless approached primarily the lowest social strata, but certainly also some of the well-to-do and of the educated people, especially merchants who through their wanderings and travels became decidedly significant in the spread of Christianity.[40] But until well into the second century, a substantial element in the communities belonged to the lower classes and there became the great majority. This is shown by certain passages from the original literature, which, like the Epistle of James or the Book of Revelation, breathe flaming hatred for the powerful and the rich. The artless form of such pieces of literature and the general tenor of eschatology show that "the members of the [Christian] communions of the post-apostolic period were still drawn mainly from the ranks of the poor and the unfree.[41]

[39] J. Weiss, op. cit., p. 132.

[40] Cf. Knopf, op. cit., p. 70.

[41] Knopf, op. cit., pp. 69 ff. The admonitions of St. Hippolytus still reveal the ethical rigorism and the hostility to middle-class life, as is seen in chapter 41 (cited by Harnack, *Die Mission und Ausbreitung des Christentums*, 1923, Vol. I, 300): "Inquiry shall likewise be made about the professions and trades of those who are brought to be admitted to the faith. If a man is a pander, he must desist or be rejected. If a man is a sculptor or painter, he must be charged not to make idols; if he does not desist, he must be rejected. If a man is an actor or pantomimist, he must desist or be rejected. A teacher of young children had best desist, but if he has no other occupation, he may be permitted to continue. A charioteer, likewise, who races or frequents races, must desist or be rejected. A gladiator or a trainer of gladiators, or a huntsman (in the wild-beast shows), or anyone connected with these shows, or a public official in charge of gladiatorial exhibitions, must desist or be rejected. A soldier of the civil authority must be taught not to kill men and to refuse to do so if he is commanded, and to refuse to take an oath; if he is unwilling to comply, he must be rejected. A

About the middle of the second century, Christianity began to win followers among the middle and higher classes of the Roman Empire. Above all, it was women of prominent position, and merchants, who took charge of the propaganda; Christianity spread in their circles and then gradually penetrated the circles of the ruling aristocracy. By the end of the second century, Christianity had already ceased to be the religion of the poor artisans and slaves. And when under Constantine it became the state religion, it had already become the religion of larger circles of the ruling class in the Roman Empire.[42]

military commander or civic magistrate that wears the purple must resign or be rejected. If a catechumen or a believer seeks to become a soldier, they must be rejected, for they have despised God. A harlot or licentious man or one who has emasculated himself, or any other who does things not to be named, must be rejected, for they are defiled. An enchanter, a diviner, a soothsayer, a user of magic verses, a juggler, a mountebank, an amulet-maker, must desist or be rejected. A concubine, who is a slave and has reared her children and has been faithful to her master alone, may become a hearer; but if she has failed in these matters she must be rejected. If a man has a concubine, he must desist and marry legally; if he is unwilling, he must be rejected. If, now, we have omitted anything, the facts will instruct your mind; for we all have the Spirit of God."

[42] As an example of the character of the community in Rome, Knopf gives a picture of the development of the social composition of the Christian church in the first three centuries. Paul, in the Epistle to the Philippians (4:22), asks that his greeting be conveyed "especially to those of Caesar's household". The fact that the death sentences imposed by Nero upon the Christians (mentioned by Tacitus, *Annales*, xv, 44), such as being sewed up in hides, dog-baiting, crucifixion, being made into living torches, might be used against only *humiliores* and not against *honestiores* (the more prominent), shows that the Christians of this period belonged mainly to the lower ranks, even though individual rich and prominent people may already have joined them. How greatly the composition of the post-apostolic church had changed is shown by a passage cited by Knopf from *I Clement*, 38:2, "the rich should offer help to the poor and the poor man should thank God that He has given him someone through whom his need can be helped". One does not observe here any trace of that animosity against the rich which pervades other documents. This is the way in which one can speak in a church where richer and more prominent people are not so very rare and

Two hundred and fifty to three hundred years after the birth of Christianity, the adherents of this faith were quite different from the first Christians. They were no longer Jews with the belief, held more passionately than by any other people, in a

also where they perform their duties to the poor (Knopf, op. cit., p. 65). From the fact that in A.D. 96, eight months before his death, Domitian had his cousin, Consul Titus Flavius, executed, and sent the cousin's first wife into exile (punishing him probably and the woman certainly on account of their adherence to Christianity), shows that already at the end of the first century, Christians in Rome had penetrated into the emperor's household. The growing number of rich and prominent Christians naturally created tensions and differences in the churches. One of these differences arose early, as to whether Christian masters should free their Christian slaves. This is shown by Paul's exhortation that slaves should not seek emancipation. But since in the course of its development, Christianity became more and more the faith of the ruling groups, these tensions were bound to grow. "The rich did not fraternize any too well with the slaves, the emancipated and the proletarians, especially in public. The poor for their part see the rich as belonging half to the devil" (Knopf, op. cit., p. 81). Hermas gives a good picture of the changed social composition. "Those who do much business also sin much, being engrossed in their business, and serving their Lord in nothing" (Sim. VIII, 9). "These are they who were faithful, but became rich and in honour among the heathen; then they put on great haughtiness and became high-minded, and abandoned the truth, and did cleave to the righteous, but lived together with the heathen, and this way pleased them better" (Sim. IX, 1). "The rich cleave with difficulty to the servants of God, fearing that they will be asked for something by them" (Sim. XX, 2). It would appear that only in the times after the Antonines did the rich and prominent, the people of blood and means, join the Christian church, as rightly understood by Eusebius in a familiar passage where he says that "during the reign of Commodus the affair [of the Christians] took an easier turn, and, thanks to the divine grace, peace embraced the churches throughout the whole world . . . insomuch that already large numbers even of those at Rome, highly distinguished for wealth and birth, were advancing towards their own salvation with all their households and kindred" (Eusebius, *Ecclesiastical History*, Book V, 21, 1). Thus in the main metropolis of the world, Christianity had ceased to be a religion primarily of poor people and slaves. From then on its power of attraction appeared in the different ranks of property and education.

messianic time soon to come. They were, rather, Greeks, Romans, Syrians, and Gauls—in short, members of all the nations of the Roman Empire. More important than this shift in nationality was the social difference. Indeed, slaves, artisans, and the shabby *proletariat*, that is, the masses of the lower classes, still constituted the bulk of the Christian communion, but Christianity had simultaneously become the religion also of the prominent and ruling classes of the Roman Empire.

In connexion with this change in the social structure of the Christian churches we must glance at the general economic and political situation of the Roman Empire, which had undergone a fundamental change during the same period. The national differences within the world empire had been steadily disappearing. Even an alien could become a Roman citizen (Edict of Caracalla, 212). At the same time, the emperor cult functioned as a unifying bond levelling national differences. The economic development was characterized by a process of gradual but progressive feudalization.

> The new relationships, as they were consolidated after the end of the third century, no longer knew any free work, but only compulsory work in the status groups (or estates) that had become hereditary, in the rural population and the colonies, as well as with the artisans and the guilds, and also (as is well known) with the patricians who had become the principal bearers of the tax burden. Thus the circle was completed. The development comes back to the point from which it has started. The medieval order is being established.[43]

The political expression of this declining economy, which was regressing into a new estate-bound "natural economy", was

[43] Eduard Meyer, "Sklaverei im Altertum", *Kleine Schriften*, 2nd ed., 1924, Vol. 1, 81.

the absolute monarchy as it was shaped by Diocletian and Constantine. A hierarchical system was developed with infinite dependencies, at the apex of which was the person of the divine emperor, to whom the masses were to render reverence and love. In a relatively short time the Roman Empire became a feudal class state with a rigidly established order in which the lowest ranks could not expect to rise because the stagnation due to the recession of productive powers made a progressive development impossible. The social system was stabilized and was regulated from the top, and it all depended on making it easier for the individual who stood at the bottom to be content with his situation.

In the main this was the social situation in the Roman Empire from the beginning of the third century on. The transformation which Christianity, especially the concept of Christ and of his relation to God the Father, underwent from its early days down to this era, must be understood primarily in the light of this social change and of the psychic change conditioned by it, and of the new sociological function which Christianity had to assume. One completely misses the vital element in the situation, therefore, if one says that "the" Christian religion spread and won over to its thinking the great majority of the population of the Roman Empire. The truth is, rather, that the original religion was transformed into another one, but the new Catholic religion had good reason for concealing this transformation.

We shall now point out what transformation Christianity underwent during the first three centuries, and show how the new religion contrasted with the old.

The most important point is that the eschatological expectations which had constituted the centre of the faith and hope of the early community gradually disappeared. The core of the missionary preaching of the early communion was, "The kingdom of God is at hand." People had prepared for the kingdom, they had even expected to experience it themselves, and they doubted whether in the short time available before the coming of the new kingdom, it would be possible to proclaim the Christian message to the majority of the heathen world. Paul's faith is still imbued with eschatological hopes, but with him the expected time of the kingdom's coming already began to be postponed further into the future. For him the final consummation was assured by the elevation of the Messiah and the last struggle, which was still to come, lost its significance in view of what had already happened. But in the subsequent development, belief in the immediate establishment of the kingdom tended more and more to disappear: "What we perceive is, rather, that unless there was a sudden spurt, the gradual disappearance of an original element, the Enthusiastic and Apocalyptic element, that is, of the sure consciousness of an immediate possession of the Divine Spirit, and the hope of the future conquering the present."[44]

If the two conceptions, the eschatological and the spiritual, were closely bound together at the beginning, with the main stress on the eschatological conception, they gradually became separated. The eschatological hope gradually receded, the nucleus of the Christian faith drew away from the second advent of Christ, and "it would then necessarily be found in the first

[44] Harnack, *History of Dogma*, New York, 1961, I, 49. Harnack emphasizes that originally two interrelated views prevailed regarding the purpose of the coming of Christ or the nature and means of salvation. Salvation, that is to say, was conceived, on the one hand, as sharing in the glorious kingdom of Christ soon to appear, and everything else was regarded as preparatory to this sure prospect; on the other hand, however, attention was turned to the conditions and to the provisions of God wrought by Christ, which first made men capable of attaining that portion, that is, of becoming sure of it. Forgiveness of sin, righteousness, faith, knowledge, etc., are the things which come into consideration here, and these blessings themselves, so far as they have as their sure result life in the kingdom of Christ, or, more accurately, eternal life, may be regarded as salvation (Harnack, op. cit., pp. 129–30).

advent, in virtue of which salvation was already prepared for man and man for salvation."[45]

The process of propagating the early Christian enthusiasm and of suppressing it, which characterized the second century, quickly died out. To be sure, there were then, as well as throughout the later history of Christianity (from the Montanists to the Anabaptists), continual attempts to revive the old Christian enthusiasm with its eschatological expectation—attempts that emanated from those groups who in their economic, social, and psychic situation, because they were oppressed and striving for freedom, resembled the first Christians. But the Church was through with these revolutionary attempts, ever since she had, in the course of the second century, won the first decisive victory. From that time on, the burden of the message was not in the cry, "The kingdom is at hand," in the expectation that Judgment Day and the return of Jesus would come soon; the Christians no longer looked to the future or to history, but, rather, they looked backward. The decisive event had already taken place. The appearance of Jesus had already represented the miracle. The real, historical world no longer needed to change; outwardly everything could remain as it was—state, society, law, economy—for salvation had become an inward, spiritual, unhistorical, individual matter guaranteed by faith in Jesus. The hope for real, historical deliverance was replaced by faith in the already complete spiritual deliverance. The historical interest was supplanted by the cosmological interest. Hand in hand with it, ethical demands faded away. The first century of Christianity was characterized by rigorous ethical postulates in the belief that the Christian community was primarily a fellowship of holy living. This practical, ethical rigorism is replaced by the means of grace dispensed by the Church. Very closely connected with the renunciation of the original rigorous ethical practice was the

[45] Harnack, ibid., p. 130.

growing reconciliation of Christians with the state. "The second century of the existence of the Christian Church already exhibits along all lines a development which moves toward a reconciliation with the state and society."[46] Even the occasional persecutions of the Christians by the state did not in the least affect this development. Although there were attempts here and there to maintain the old rigorist ethic hostile to the state and middle-class life, the great majority of Christians, especially the leading bishops, decided differently. It now sufficed to have God in one's heart and to confess faith in Him when a public confession before the authorities was unavoidable. It was enough to flee the actual worship of idols, otherwise the Christian could remain in every honourable calling; there he was allowed to come into external contact with the worship of idols, and he should conduct himself prudently and cautiously so that he neither contaminated himself nor even ran the risk of contaminating himself and others. The Church adopted this attitude everywhere after the beginning of the third century. The state thereby gained numerous quiet, dutiful, and conscientious citizens who, far from causing it any difficulty, supported order and peace in society. . . . Since the Church had abandoned her rigid, negative attitude towards the world, she developed into a state-supporting and state-reforming power. If we may introduce a modern phenomenon for comparison, we may say that the world-fleeing fanatics who awaited the heavenly state of the future became revisionists of the existing order of life.[47]

This fundamental transformation of Christianity from the religion of the oppressed to the religion of the rulers—and of the masses manipulated by them, from the expectation of the imminent approach of Judgment Day and the new age to a faith

[46] Harnack, "Kirche und Staat bis zur Gründung der Staatskirche", *Kultur der Gegenwart*, and ed., Vol. I, 4, 1, p. 239.
[47] Harnack, ibid., p. 143.

in the already consummated redemption; from the postulate of a pure, moral life to satisfaction of conscience through ecclesiastical means of grace; from hostility to the hated state to cordial agreement with it—all this is closely connected with the final great change about to be described. Christianity, which had been the religion of a community of equal brothers, without hierarchy or bureaucracy, became "the Church", the reflected image of the absolute monarchy of the Roman Empire.

In the first century there was not even a clearly defined external authority in the Christian communities, which were accordingly built upon the independence and freedom of the individual Christian with respect to matters of faith. The second century was characterized by the gradual development of an ecclesiastical union with authoritative leaders and thus, also, by the establishment of a systematic doctrine of faith to which the individual Christian had to submit. Originally it was not the Church but God alone who could forgive sins. Later, *Extra ecclesiam nulla salus*; the Church alone offers protection against any self-centred loss of grace. As an institution, the Church became holy by virtue of her endowment, the moral establishment that educates for salvation. This function is restricted to the priests, especially to the episcopate, "which in its unity guarantees the legitimacy of the Church and has received the jurisdiction of forgiveness of sins."[48] This transformation of the free brotherly fellowship into a hierarchical organization clearly indicates the psychic change that had occurred.[49] As the first Christians were imbued with hatred and contempt for the educated rich and the rulers, in short, for all authority, so the Christians from the third century on were imbued with reverence, love, and fidelity to the new clerical authorities.

Just as Christianity was transformed in every respect in the

[48] Cyprian, *Epistle* 69, 11.

[49] Cf. Harnack, *History of Dogma*, New York, 1961, II, pp. 67–94.

first three centuries of its existence and became a new religion as compared with the original one, this was true also with respect to the concept of Jesus. In early Christianity the adoptionist doctrine prevailed, that is, the belief that the man Jesus had been elevated to a god. With the continued development of the Church, the concept of the nature of Jesus leaned more and more toward the pneumatic viewpoint: a man was not elevated to a god, but a god descended to become a man. This is the basis of the new concept of Christ, until it culminated in the doctrine of Athanasius, which was adopted by the Nicene Council: Jesus, the son of God, born of the Father before all time, of one substance with the Father. The Arian view that Jesus and God the Father were indeed of similar but not identical substance is rejected in favour of the logically contradictory thesis that two substances, God and His Son, are only one substance; this is the assertion of a duality that is simultaneously a unity. What is the meaning of this change in the concept of Jesus and His relation to God the Father, and what relation does the change in dogma bear to the change in the whole religion?

Early Christianity was hostile to authority and to the state. It satisfied in fantasy the revolutionary wishes of the lower classes hostile to the Father. The Christianity that was elevated to the official religion of the Roman Empire three hundred years later had a completely different social function. It was intended to be, at the same time, a religion for both the leaders and the led; the rulers and the ruled. Christianity fulfilled the function which the emperor and the Mithras cult could not nearly so well fulfil, namely, the integration of the masses into the absolutist system of the Roman Empire. The revolutionary situation which had prevailed until the second century had disappeared. Economic regression had supervened; the Middle Ages began to develop. The economic situation led to a system of social ties and dependencies that came to their peak politically in the Roman-Byzantine absolutism. The new Christianity came under the leadership of the ruling class. The new dogma of Jesus was created and formulated by this ruling group and its intellectual representatives, not by the masses. The decisive element was the change from the idea of man becoming god to that of god becoming man.

Since the new concept of the Son, who was indeed a second being beside God yet one with Him, changed the tension between God and His Son into harmony, and since it avoided the concept that a man could become God, it eliminated from the formula the revolutionary character of the older doctrine, namely, hostility to the father. The Oedipus crime contained in the old formula, the displacement of the father by the son, was eliminated in the new Christianity. The father remained untouched in his position. Now, however, it was not a man, but his only begotten Son, existing before all creation, who was beside him. Jesus Himself became God without dethroning God because he had always been a component of God.

Thus far we have understood only the negative point, why Jesus could no longer be the man raised to a god, the man set at the right hand of the father. The need for recognition of the father, for passive subordination to him, could have been satisfied by the great competitor of Christianity, the emperor cult. Why did Christianity and not the emperor cult succeed in becoming the established state religion of the Roman Empire? Because Christianity had a quality that made it superior for the social function it was intended to fulfil, namely, faith in the crucified Son of God. Besides, the suffering and oppressed masses could identify with Him to a greater degree. But the fantasy satisfaction became different. The masses no longer identified with the crucified man in order to dethrone the father in fantasy, but, rather, in order to enjoy his love and grace. The idea that a man became a god was a symbol of aggressive, active, hostile-to-the-father tendencies. The idea that God became a man was transformed into a symbol of the tender, passive tie to the father. The masses found their satisfaction in the fact that their representative, the crucified Jesus, was elevated in status, becoming Himself a pre-existent god. People no longer expected an imminent historical change but believed, rather, that deliverance had already taken place, that what they hoped for had already happened. They rejected the fantasy which represented hostility to the father, and accepted another in its place, the harmonizing one of the son placed beside the father by the latter's free will. This is the core meaning contained in the logical contradiction of the dogma of the Trinity.[50]

The logical contradiction is the expression of a sociological one, that is, the change in the social function of Christianity. Far from being a religion of rebels and revolutionaries, this religion of the ruling class was now determined to keep the masses on leashes and lead them. Since the old revolutionary representative was retained, however, the emotional need of the masses was satisfied in a new way. The formula of passive submission replaced the active hostility to the father. It was not necessary to displace the father, since the son had indeed been equal to God from the beginning precisely because God Himself had "emitted" him. The actual possibility of identifying with a god who had suffered yet had from the beginning been in heaven, and at the same time of eliminating tendencies hostile to the father, is the basis for the victory of Christianity over the emperor cult. Moreover, the change in the attitude toward the real, existing father figures—the priests, the emperor, and especially the rulers—corresponded to this changed attitude toward the father-god.

The psychic situation of the Catholic masses of the fourth century was unlike that of the early Christians in that the hatred

[50] We can leave out of consideration the third member of the Trinity, the Holy Ghost. The Trinity was originally a binitarian dogma and arose from the combination of two formulas for it.

for the rulers, including the father-god, was no longer conscious, or was only relatively so; the people had given up their revolutionary attitude. The reason for this lies in the change of the social reality. Every hope for the overthrow of the rulers and for the victory of their own class was so hopeless that, from the psychic viewpoint, it would have been futile and uneconomical to persist in the attitude of hatred. If it was hopeless to overthrow the father, then the better psychic escape was to submit to him, to love him, and to receive love from him. This change of psychic attitude was the inevitable result of the final defeat of the oppressed class.

But the aggressive impulses could not have disappeared. Nor could they even have diminished, for their real cause, the oppression by the rulers, was neither removed nor reduced. Where were the aggressive impulses now? They were turned away from the earlier objects—the fathers, the authorities—and directed back toward the individual self. The identification with the suffering, crucified Jesus offered a magnificent opportunity for this. In Catholic dogma the stress was no longer, as in the early Christian doctrine, on the overthrow of the father but on the self-annihilation of the son. The original aggression directed against the father was turned against the self, and it thereby provided an outlet that was harmless for social stability.

But this was possible only in connexion with another change. For the first Christians, the rulers and the rich were the evil people who would reap the deserved reward for their wickedness. Certainly the early Christians were not without guilt feelings on account of their hostility to the father; and the identification with the suffering Jesus had also served to expiate their aggression; but without doubt the emphasis for them was not in the guilt feelings and the masochistic, atoning reaction. For the Catholic masses later on the situation had changed. For them no longer were the rulers to blame for wretchedness and suffering; rather, the sufferers themselves were guilty. They must reproach themselves if they are unhappy. Only through constant expiation, only through personal suffering could they atone for their guilt and win the love and pardon of God and of His earthly representatives. By suffering and castrating oneself, one finds an escape from the oppressive guilt feeling and has a chance to receive pardon and love.[51]

The Catholic Church understood how to accelerate and strengthen in a masterful way this process of changing the reproach against God and the rulers into reproach of the self. It increased the guilt feeling of the masses to a point where it was almost unbearable; and in doing so it achieved a double purpose: first, it helped turn reproaches and aggression away from the ruling classes and toward the suffering masses; and, second, it offered itself to these suffering masses as a good and loving father, since the priests granted pardon and expiation for the guilt feeling which they themselves had engendered. It ingeniously cultivated the psychic condition from which it, and the upper class, derived a double advantage; the diversion of the aggression of the masses and the assurance of their dependency, gratitude, and love.

For the rulers, however, the fantasy of the suffering Jesus had not only this social function but also an important psychic function. It relieved them of the guilt feelings they experienced because of the distress and suffering of the masses whom they had oppressed and exploited. By identifying with the suffering Jesus, the exploiting groups could themselves do penance. They could comfort themselves with the idea that, since even God's only begotten Son had suffered voluntarily, suffering for the masses was a grace of God, and therefore they had no reason to reproach themselves for causing such suffering.

The transformation of Christological dogma, as well as that of

[51] Cf. Freud's remarks in *Civilization and its Discontents* (Standard edition, XXI), pp. 123 ff.

the whole Christian religion, merely corresponded to the sociological function of religion in general, the maintenance of social stability by preserving the interests of the ruling class. For the first Christians it was a blessed and satisfying dream to create the fantasy that the hated authorities would soon be overthrown and that they themselves, now poor and suffering, would achieve mastery and happiness. After their final defeat, and after all their expectations had proved futile, the masses became satisfied with a fantasy in which they accepted responsibility for all suffering; they could, however, atone for their sins through their own suffering and then hope to be loved by a good father. He had proved himself a loving father when, in the form of the son, He became a suffering man. Their other wishes for happiness, and not merely forgiveness, were satisfied in the fantasy of a blissful hereafter, a hereafter which was supposed to replace the historically happy condition in this world which the early Christians had hoped for.

In our interpretation of the Homoousian formula, however, we have not yet found its unique and ultimate unconscious meaning. Analytic experience leads us to expect that behind the logical contradiction of the formula, namely, that two are equal to one, must be hidden a specific unconscious meaning to which the dogma owes its significance and its fascination. This most profound, unconscious meaning of the Homoousian doctrine becomes clear when we recall a simple fact: there is one actual situation in which this formula makes sense, the situation of the child in its mother's womb. Mother and child are then two beings and at the same time are one.

We have now arrived at the central problem of the change in the idea of the relation of Jesus to God the Father. Not only the son has changed but the father as well. The strong, powerful father has become the sheltering and protecting mother; the once rebellious, then suffering and passive son has become the small child. Under the guise of the fatherly God of the Jews, who in the struggle with the Near Eastern motherly divinities had gained dominance, the divine figure of the Great Mother emerges again, and becomes the dominating figure of medieval Christianity.

The significance that the motherly divinity had for Catholic Christianity from the fourth century on becomes clear, first, in the role that the Church, as such, begins to play; and second, in the cult of Mary.[52] It has been shown that for early Christianity the idea of a *church* was still quite alien. Only in the course of historical development does the Church gradually assume a hierarchical organization; the Church itself becomes a holy institution and more than merely the sum of its members. The Church mediates salvation; the believers are her children; she is the Great Mother through whom alone man can achieve security and blessedness.

Equally revealing is the revival of the figure of the motherly divinity in the cult of Mary. Mary represents that motherly divinity grown independent by separating itself from the fathergod. In her, the motherly qualities, which had always unconsciously been a part of the God the Father, were now consciously and clearly experienced and symbolically represented.

In the New Testament account, Mary was in no way elevated beyond the sphere of ordinary men. With the development of Christology, ideas about Mary assumed an ever-increasing prominence. The more the figure of the historical human Jesus retreated in favour of the pre-existent Son of God, the more Mary was deified. Although, according to the New Testament, Mary in her marriage with Joseph continued to bear children, Epiphanius disputed that view as heretical and frivolous. In the Nestorian controversy a decision against Nestorius was reached in 431 that Mary was not only the mother of Christ but also the mother of God, and at the end of the fourth century there arose a

[52] Cf. A. J. Storfer, *Marias jungfräuliche Mutterschaft*, Berlin, 1913.

cult of Mary, and men addressed prayers to her. About the same time the representation of Mary in the plastic arts also began to play a great and ever-increasing role. The succeeding centuries attached more and more significance to the mother of God, and her worship became more exuberant and more general. Altars were erected to her, and her pictures were shown everywhere. From a recipient of grace she became the dispenser of grace with a benignity not even attributed to Christ himself.[53] Mary with the infant Jesus became the symbol of the Catholic Middle Ages.

The full significance of the collective fantasy of the nursing Madonna becomes clear only through the results of psychoanalytic clinical investigations. Sándor Radó has pointed out the extraordinary significance which the fear of starvation, on the one hand, and the happiness of oral satisfaction, on the other, play in the psychic life of the individual:

> The torments of hunger become a psychic foretaste of later "punishments" and through the school of punishment they become the primitive mechanism of a self-punishment which finally in melancholia achieves so fateful a significance. Behind the boundless fear of pauperization felt by the melancholy is hidden nothing other than the fear of starvation (i.e., the fear of becoming a pauper in a physiological sense, i.e., in physiological equipment); this fear is the reaction of the vitality of the normal ego-residue to the life-threatening, melancholic act of

[53] The connexion of the worship of Mary with the worship of the pagan mother divinities has been dealt with a number of times. A particularly clear example is found in the Collyridians, who, as priestesses of Mary, carried cakes about in a solemn procession on a day consecrated to her, similar to the cult of the Canaanite queen of heaven mentioned by Jeremiah. Cf. Rösch (*Th. St. K.*, 1888, pp. 278 f.), who interprets the cake as a phallic symbol and views the Mary worshipped by the Collyridians as identical with the Oriental-Phoenician Astarte (see *Realenzyklopädie für protestantische Theologie und Kirche*, Vol. XII, Leipzig, 1915).

> expiation of penance imposed by the Church. Drinking from the breast, however, remains the shining example of the unfailing, pardoning proffer of love. It is certainly no accident that the nursing Madonna with the child has become the symbol of a powerful religion and through her mediation the symbol of a whole epoch of our Western culture. In my opinion, the derivation of the meaning-complex of Guilt-Atonement-Pardon from the early infantile experience of Rage-Hunger-Drinking from the breast solves our riddle as to why the hope for absolution and love is perhaps the most powerful configuration we encounter in the higher levels of human psychic life.[54]

Radó's study makes entirely intelligible the connexion between the fantasy of the suffering Jesus and that of the child Jesus on the mother's breast. Both fantasies are an expression of the wish for pardon and expiation. In the fantasy of the crucified Jesus, pardon is obtained by a passive, self-castrating submission to the father. In the fantasy of the child Jesus on the breast of the Madonna the masochistic element is lacking; in place of the father one finds the mother who, while she pacifies the child, grants pardon and expiation. The same happy feeling constitutes the unconscious meaning of the Homoousian dogma, the fantasy of the child sheltered in the womb.

This fantasy of the great pardoning mother is the optimal gratification which Catholic Christianity had to offer to the fantasy of the masses. The more the masses suffered, the more their real situation resembled that of the suffering Jesus, and the more the figure of the happy suckling babe could, and must, appear alongside the figure of the suffering Jesus. But this meant also that men had to regress to a passive, infantile attitude. This position precluded active revolt; it was the psychic attitude corresponding to the man of hierarchically structured medieval

[54] *Internationale Zeitschrift für Psychoanalyse*, XIII, p. 445.

society, a human being who found himself dependent on the rulers, who expected to secure from them his minimum sustenance, and for whom hunger was proof of his sins.

5. THE DEVELOPMENT OF THE DOGMA UNTIL THE NICENE COUNCIL

Thus far we have followed the changes in the concepts of Christ and His relation to God the Father from their beginning in the early Christian faith to the Nicene dogma, and have tried to point out the motives for the changes. The development had several intermediate stages, however, which are characterized by the different formulations that appeared down to the Nicene Council. This development proceeds by contradiction, and this can be understood dialectically only together with the gradual evolution of Christianity from a revolutionary into a state-supporting religion. To demonstrate that the different formulations of the dogma correspond at each time to a particular class and its needs, constitutes a special study. Nevertheless, the basic features should be indicated here.

Second-century Christianity, which had already begun its "revisionism", was characterized by a battle on two fronts: on the one hand, the revolutionary tendencies which still flared up with some force in widely different places had to be suppressed; on the other hand, tendencies which were inclined to develop too quickly in the direction of social conformity, indeed more quickly than the social development permitted, also had to be suppressed. The masses could take only a slow, gradual course from the hope in a revolutionary Jesus to faith in a state-supporting Jesus.

The strongest expression of early Christian tendencies was Montanism. Originally the powerful effort of a Phrygian prophet, Montanus, in the second half of the second century, Montanism was a reaction against the conforming tendencies of

Christianity, a reaction that sought to restore the early Christian enthusiasm. Montanus wished to withdraw the Christians from their social relationships and to establish through his followers a new community apart from the world, a community that was to prepare itself for the descent of the "upper Jerusalem". Montanism was a flare-up of the early Christian mood, but the transformation process of Christianity had already gone so far that this revolutionary tendency was fought as heresy by the Church authorities, who acted like bailiffs of the Roman state. (The behaviour of Luther toward the revolting peasants and Anabaptists was similar in many respects.)

The Gnostics, on the other hand, were the intellectual representatives of the well-to-do Hellenistic middle class. According to Harnack, Gnosticism represented the "acute secularising" of Christianity, and anticipates a development which had to continue for another one hundred and fifty years. At that moment it was attacked by the official Church, along with Montanism, but only an undialectical interpretation can overlook the fact that the struggle of the Church against Montanism was very different in character from that against Gnosticism. Montanism was resisted because it was the resurgence of a movement which had already been subdued and which was dangerous for the present leaders of Christianity. Gnosticism was resisted because it wanted to accomplish too quickly and too suddenly what it wished, since it announced the secret of the coming Christian development before the consciousness of the masses could accept it.

The Gnostic ideas of faith, especially their Christological and eschatological conceptions, correspond exactly with the expectations which we must have on the basis of our study of the social-psychological background of dogmatic development. It is not surprising that Gnosticism denies entirely the early Christian eschatology, especially the second coming of Christ and the resurrection of the flesh, and expects of the future only the freeing of the spirit from its material covering. This thorough rejection of eschatology, which was achieved in Catholicism a hundred and fifty years later, was at that time premature; eschatological concepts were still ideologically retained by the Apologists, who in other respects had already become widely separated from the early Christian conception. Such a remnant was judged "archaic" by Harnack, but necessary at that time for the satisfaction of the masses.

Another doctrine of Gnosticism closely connected with this rejection of eschatology should be noted: that is, the Gnostic stress on the discrepancy between the supreme God and the creator of the world, and the assertion that "the present world sprang from a fall of man, or from an undertaking hostile to God, and is, therefore, the product of an evil or intermediate being".[55] The meaning of this thesis is clear: if creation, that is, the historical world, as it finds expression in social and political life, is evil from the beginning, if it is the work of an intermediary, indifferent, or feeble God, then indeed it cannot be redeemed, and all the early Christian eschatological hopes must be false and unfounded. Gnosticism rejected the real collective change and redemption of humanity, and substituted an individual ideal of knowledge, dividing men along religious and spiritual lines into definite classes and castes; social and economic divisions were regarded as good and God-given. Men were divided into pneumatics, who enjoyed the highest blessedness; psychics, who shared somewhat lesser blessedness; and hylics, who had fallen completely into decline. It was a rejection of collective redemption and an assertion of the class stratification of society like that which Catholicism established later in the separation of laity from clergy, and the life of the common people from that of the monks.

What then was the concept of the Gnostics concerning Jesus and His relation to God the Father? They taught that

[55] Harnack, *History of Dogma*, New York, 1961, I, p. 258.

> the heavenly Aeon, Christ, and the human appearance of that Aeon must be clearly distinguished, and a "distincte agere" ascribed to each. . . . There were some, such as Basilides, who acknowledged no real union between Christ and the man Jesus, whom, besides, they regarded as an earthly man. Others, e.g., part of the Valentinians . . . taught that the body of Jesus was a heavenly psychical formation, and sprang from the womb of Mary only in appearance. Finally, a third party, such as Saturinus, declared that the whole visible appearance of Christ was a phantom, and therefore denied the birth of Christ.[56]

What is the meaning of these conceptions? The decisive feature is that the original Christian idea that a real man (whose character as a revolutionary and as one hostile to the father we have already set forth) became a god is eliminated. The different Gnostic tendencies are only expressions of the different possibilities of this elimination. All of them deny that Christ was a real man, thus maintaining the inviolability of the father-god. The connexion with the concept of redemption is also clear. It is just as unlikely that this world, which is by nature evil, can become good, as it is that a real man can become a god; this means that it is equally unlikely that there is anything in the existing social situation that can be changed. It is a misunderstanding to believe that the Gnostics' thesis—that God the Creator of the Old Testament is not the highest God, but an inferior god—is an expression of especially hostile tendencies to the father. The Gnostics had to assert the inferiority of God the Creator in order to demonstrate the thesis of the immutability of the world and of human society, but for them this assertion was therefore not an expression of hostility to the father. Their thesis, in contrast to the first Christians, dealt with a god alien to them, the Jewish Jahwe, whom these Greeks had no reason to respect. For them,

[56] Harnack, *History of Dogma*, New York, 1961, pp. 259–260.

to dethrone this Jewish deity neither entailed nor presupposed any special hostile emotions toward the father.

The Catholic Church, which fought Montanism as a dangerous remnant and Gnosticism as a premature anticipation of what was to come, moved gradually but steadily toward the final achievement of her goal in the fourth century. The Apologists were first to provide the theory for this development. They created dogmas—they were the first to use this term in the technical sense—in which the changed attitude toward God and society found expression. To be sure, they were not so radical as the Gnostics: it has been pointed out that they retained the eschatological ideas and thus served as a link with early Christianity. Their doctrine of Jesus and his relation to God the Father, however, was closely related to the Gnostic position and contained the seed of the Nicene dogma. They attempted to present Christianity as the highest philosophy; they "formulated the content of the Gospel in a manner which appealed to the common sense of all serious thinkers and intelligent men of the age"[57] [that is, the middle and upper classes. E.F.].

Though the apologists did not teach that matter is evil, they did not, however, make God the direct originator of the world, but personified divine intelligence and inserted it between God and the world. One thesis, though less radical than the corresponding Gnostic one, has the same opposition to historical redemption. The Logos, ejected by God out of himself for the purpose of creation, and produced by a voluntary act, was for them the Son of God. On the one hand, he was not separated from God but was rather the result of God's own unfolding; on the other hand, he was God and Lord, his personality had a beginning, he was creature in relation to God; yet his subordination lay not in his nature but rather in his origination.

[57] Harnack, *History of Dogma*, New York, 1961, II, p. 110.

This Logos Christology of the apologists was in essence identical with the Nicene dogma. The adoptionist, anti-authoritarian theory concerning the man who became God was discarded, and Jesus became the pre-existent only-begotten Son of God, of one nature with him and yet a second being beside him. Our interpretation of this source of the Nicene doctrine therefore holds, in essence, for the Logos Christology, which was the decisive precursor of the new Catholic Christianity.

> The assimilation of the Logos Christology into the faith of the Church . . . involved a transformation of faith into doctrine with Greek-philosophical features; it pushed back the old eschatological ideas; indeed, it suppressed them; it substituted for the Christ of history a conceptual Christ, a principle, and transformed the historical Christ into phenomena. It led Christians to "Nature" and to naturalistic greatness, instead of to the personal and the moral; it gave to the faith of the Christians definitely the direction toward the contemplation of ideas and dogmas, thus preparing the way, on the one hand, for the monastic life, and, on the other, for a tutored Christianity of imperfect, working laymen. It legitimized hundreds of questions of cosmology and of the nature of the world as religious questions, and it demanded a definite answer on pain of losing salvation. This led to a situation where, instead of preaching faith, people preached faith in the faith and stunted religion while ostensibly enlarging it. But since it perfected the alliance with science, it shaped Christianity into a world-religion, and indeed into a cosmopolitan religion, and prepared the way for the Act of Constantine.[58]

Thus in the Logos Christology the seed of the definitive Christian-Catholic dogma was created. Its recognition and adop-

[58] Harnack, *Lehrbuch der Dogmengeschichte*, 6th ed., 1922, p. 155.

tion did not proceed, however, without a severe struggle against ideas which contradicted it, behind which were hidden remnants of early Christian views and the early Christian mood. The concept has been called *monarchianism* (first by Tertullian). Within monarchianism two tendencies can be distinguished: the adoptionist and the modalist. Adoptionist monarchianism started with Jesus as a human who became God. The modalist view held that Jesus was only a manifestation of God the Father, not a god alongside him. Both tendencies were, therefore, monarchian in that they asserted the monarchy of God: one, that a man was inspired by the divine spirit, while God remained inviolable as a unique being; the other, that the Son was only a manifestation of the Father, again preserving the monarchy of God. Although the two branches of monarchianism appeared to contradict each other, the contrast was actually much less sharp. Harnack points out that the two views, apparently so opposed, in many ways coincide, and psychoanalytic interpretation makes fully intelligible the affinity of the two monarchian movements. It has already been indicated that the unconscious meaning of the adoptionist conception is the wish to displace the father-god; if a man can become God and be enthroned at the right hand of God, then God is in reality dethroned. However, the same tendency is clear in the modalist dogma; if Jesus was only a manifestation of God, then certainly God the Father Himself was crucified, suffered, and died—a view that has been called *Patripassianism*. In this modalistic conception we recognize a clear affinity with the old Near Eastern myths of the dying god (Attis, Adonis, Osiris), which imply an unconscious hostility to the father-god.

It is precisely the reverse of what an interpretation which disregarded the psychic situation of the people supporting the dogma might believe. Monarchianism, adoptionist as well as modalist, signifies not an increased reverence for God but the opposite—the wish for His displacement, which is expressed in the deification of a man or in the crucifixion of God Himself.

From what has already been said, it is fully understandable that Harnack emphasizes, as one of the essential points on which the two monarchian movements agree, the fact that they represented the eschatological as opposed to the naturalistic conception of the person of Christ. We have seen that the former idea, that Jesus will return to establish the new kingdom, was an essential part of primitive Christian belief, which was revolutionary and hostile to the father. We are therefore not surprised to find this conception also in the two monarchian movements, whose relationship to early Christian doctrine has been demonstrated. Nor are we surprised that Tertullian and Origen testified that the bulk of the Christian people thought in monarchian terms, and we understand that the struggle against both types of monarchianism was essentially an expression of the struggle against the tendencies, still rooted in the masses, of hostility to the father-god and to the state.

We pass over individual nuances within dogmatic development and turn to the great disagreement which found a preliminary settlement in the Nicene Council, namely, the controversy between Arius and Athanasius. Arius taught that God is One, beside whom there is no other, and that his Son was an independent being quite different in essence from the Father. Nor did he possess the same essence as the Father; he was not true God and he had divine qualities only as acquired ones, and only in part. Because he was not eternal, his knowledge was not perfect. Therefore, he was not entitled to the same honour as the Father. But he was created before the world, as an instrument for the creation of other creatures, having been created by the will of God as an independent being. Athanasius contrasted the Son, who belonged to God, with the world: he was produced from the essence of God, shared completely the whole nature of the Father, had one and the same essence with the Father, and forms with God a strict unity.

We can easily recognize behind the opposition between Arius

and Athanasius the old controversy between the monarchian conception and the Logos Christology of the apologists (even though Athanasius made minor changes in the old Logos doctrine through new formulations), the struggle between the revolutionary tendencies hostile to the father-god and the conformist movement supporting father and state, and renouncing a collective and historical liberation. The latter finally triumphed in the fourth century, when Christianity became the official religion of the Roman Empire. Arius, a pupil of Lucian, who was in turn a pupil of Paul of Samosata, one of the outstanding proponents of adoptionism, represented adoptionism no longer in its pure, original form but already mixed with elements of the Logos Christology. That could not be otherwise, for the development of Christianity away from the early enthusiasm and toward the Catholic Church had already progressed so far that the old opposition could be fought out only in the language and in the climate of ecclesiastical views. If the controversy between Athanasius and Arius seemed to revolve around a small difference (whether God and His Son are of the same substance or of like substance, *Homoousion* or *Homoiousion*), the smallness of this difference was precisely the consequence of the victory, now nearly complete, over the early Christian tendencies. But behind this debate lay nothing less than the conflict between revolutionary and reactionary tendencies. The Arian dogma was one of the final convulsions of the early Christian movement; the victory of Athanasius sealed the defeat of the religion and the hopes of the small peasants, artisans, and proletarians in Palestine.

We have tried to show with broad strokes how the various stages in the dogmatic development were in character with the general trend of this development from the early Christian faith to the Nicene dogma. It would be an attractive task, which we must forgo in this study, to show also the social situation of the groups that were involved at each stage. It would also be worth while to study the reason why nine-tenths of the Orient and the

Germans adhered to Arianism. We believe, however, that we have shown sufficiently that the various stages of dogma development, and both its beginning and end, can be understood only on the basis of changes in the actual social situation and function of Christianity.

6. ANOTHER ATTEMPT AT INTERPRETATION

What are the differences in method and in content between the present study and that of Theodor Reik dealing with the same material?

Reik proceeds methodologically in the following manner. The special object of his investigation is dogma, particularly Christological dogma. Since he is "concerned with pursuing the parallels between religion and compulsion-neurosis and showing the connexion between the two phenomena in single examples", he tries to show, "especially in this representative example that religious dogma in the evolutionary history of humanity corresponds to neurotic obsessional thought, that it is the most significant expression of irrational compulsive thinking". The psychic processes that lead to the construction and development of dogma follow throughout the psychic mechanism of obsessional thinking, and the same motives predominate in both. "In the shaping of dogma the same defence mechanisms are involved as in the compulsive processes in the individual."

How does Reik proceed to develop his thesis concerning the fundamental analogy between dogma and compulsion?

First, on the basis of his idea of the analogy between religion and the compulsion-neurosis, he expects to find this agreement in all individual aspects of both phenomena, and therefore also between religious thinking and compulsive thinking. He then turns to the evolution of dogma and sees how it is carried out along the lines of a continued struggle over small differences; it does not seem far-fetched to assume that this striking similarity between dogmatic development and obsessional thinking is to be interpreted as proof of the identity of the two phenomena, and thus the unknown is to be explained by the known, the shaping of dogma is to be understood as following the same laws that govern compulsive-neurotic processes. The hypothesis of an inner relationship between the two phenomena is strengthened by the fact that in the Christological dogma in particular, the relation to God the Father, with its basic ambivalence, plays a striking and special role.

In Reik's methodological attitude there are certain assumptions which are not explicitly mentioned, but whose exposition is necessary for the criticism of his method. The most important is the following: because a religion, in this case Christianity, is conceived and presented as one entity, the follower of this religion is assumed to be a unified subject, and the masses are thus treated as if they were one man, an individual. Like organicistic sociology, which has conceived of society as a living entity and has understood the different groups within society as different parts of an organism, thus referring to the eyes, the skin, the head, and so on, of society, Reik adopts an organicistic concept—not in the anatomic but in the psychological sense. Furthermore, he does not attempt to investigate the masses, whose unity he assumes, in their real life situation. He assumes the masses are identical, and deals only with the ideas and ideologies produced by the masses, not concerning himself concretely with living men and their psychic situation. He does not interpret the ideologies as produced by men; he reconstructs the men from the ideologies. Consequently his method is relevant for the history of dogma and not a method for the study of religious and social history. Thus it is quite similar not only to organicistic sociology but also to a method of religious research oriented surely to the history of ideas, which has already been abandoned even by many historians of religion, for example, Harnack. By his method Reik implicitly supports the theological approach, which the content of his work consciously and explicitly rejects. This theological viewpoint emphasizes the unity of Christian religion—indeed, Catholicism claims immutability; and if we adopt as method the analysis of Christianity as if it were a living individual, we will, logically, be brought to the orthodox Catholic position. The element common to the two viewpoints is fundamentally the idea that man neither changes nor develops in history.

The methodology just discussed is of great significance in the investigation of Christian dogma because it is decisive for the concept of ambivalence, which is central for Reik's work. Whether the assumption of a unified subject is acceptable or not is a matter that can be decided only after an investigation—lacking in Reik—of the psychic, social, and economic situation, of the "psychic surfaces" of the group. The present study has attempted to show that this assumption would not be valid for the Christianity of that period. In that case, the application of Reik's concept of ambivalence would be untenable. The term ambivalence applies only when there is a conflict of impulses within one individual, or perhaps within a group of relatively homogeneous individuals. If a man simultaneously loves and hates another person, we can speak of ambivalence. But if, when there are two men, one loves and the other hates a third man, the two men are opponents. We can analyze why one loves and the other hates, but it would be rather confusing to speak of an ambivalence. When within a group we confront the simultaneous presence of contradictory impulses, only an investigation of the realistic situation of this group can show whether behind their apparent unity we might not find different subgroups, each with different desires, and fighting with each other. The apparent ambivalence might indeed turn out to be a conflict between different subgroups.

An example may illustrate this point. Let us imagine that in several hundred or a thousand years, a research psychoanalyst, using Reik's method, made a study of the political history of Germany after the Revolution of the 1918, and particularly the dispute over the colours of the German flag. He would establish that there were in the German nation some who favoured a black-white-red flag; others who insisted on a black-red-gold flag; and others again who wanted a red flag—and then an agreement was reached whereby it was decided to make the main flag black-red-gold, and the trade flag on ships black-white-red with a black-red-gold corner. Our imaginary analyst would first examine the rationalizations and find, perhaps, that one group wanted to keep the black-white-red flag because these colours are more visible on the ocean than black-red-gold. He would indicate what significance the attitude toward the father had in this battle (monarchy or republic), and he would go on to discover an analogy to the thinking of a compulsive neurotic. He would then cite examples where the doubt as to which colour was the right one (Reik's example of the patient who cudgelled his brains over the white or black necktie serves excellently here) is rooted in the conflict of ambivalent impulses, and would see in the fuss over the colours of the flag and in the final flag compromise a phenomenon analogous to obsessional thinking conditioned by the same causes.

No one who understands the real relationships (including even the later investigator, in so far as he does not turn his attention primarily to the competing solutions, but gives his attention to the men interested in them) will doubt that the inference from analogy would be false. It is clear that there were different groups whose different realistic and affective interests are in conflict with one another, that the struggle over the flag is a struggle between groups differently oriented both psychically and economically, and that one is concerned here with anything but an "ambivalence conflict". The flag compromise was not the result of an ambivalence conflict, but rather the compromise between different claims of social groups fighting with each other.

What substantial differences result from the methodological difference? Both in the interpretation of the content of Christological dogma and in the psychological evaluation of dogma as such, a different method leads to different results.

There is a common point of departure, the interpretation of early Christian faith as an expression of hostility to the father. In the interpretation of the further dogmatic development, however, we come to a conclusion precisely the opposite of Reik's. Reik considers Gnosticism a movement in which rebellious impulses, supported by the son-religion of Christianity, have predominated to the extreme, to the downgrading of the father-god. We have tried to show that, on the contrary, Gnosticism eliminated the early Christian revolutionary tendencies. Reik's error seems to us to grow out of the fact that, according to his method, he notices only the Gnostic formula of the removal of the Jewish father-god, instead of looking at Gnosticism as a whole, in which a quite different significance can be attributed to the formula of hostility to Jahwe. The interpretation of further dogmatic development leads to other equally contrary results. Reik sees in the doctrine of the pre-existence of Jesus the survival and conquest of the original Christian hostility to the father. In direct opposition to this idea I have tried to show that in the idea of the pre-existence of Jesus, the original hostility to the father is replaced by an opposite harmonizing tendency. We see that the psychoanalytic interpretation leads here to two opposite conceptions of the unconscious meaning of different dogma formulations. This opposition certainly does not depend upon any difference in the psychoanalytic presuppositions as such. It rests only upon the difference in the method of applying psychoanalysis to social-psychological phenomena. The conclusions to which we come seem to us to be correct because, unlike Reik's, they stem not from the interpretation of an isolated and absolutized religious formula but rather from the examination of this formula in its connexion with the real life situation of the men holding it.

No less important is our disagreement, resulting from the same methodological difference, with respect to the interpretation of the psychological significance of dogma as such. Reik sees in dogma the most significant expression of popular compulsive thought, and tries to show "that the psychic processes which lead to the establishment and development of dogma consistently follow the psychic mechanisms of compulsive thinking, that the same motives predominate in the one area as in the other". He finds the development of dogma conditioned by an ambivalent attitude toward the father. For Reik, the hostility to the father finds its first high point in Gnosticism. The apologists then develop a Logos Christology, where the unconscious purpose of replacing God the Father by Christ is clearly symbolized, although the victory of unconscious impulses is prevented by strong defence forces. Just as in a compulsive neurosis, and where two opposite tendencies alternately win the upper hand, according to Reik the same conflicting tendencies appear in the development of dogma, which follows the same laws as the neurosis. We have shown above in detail the source of Reik's error. He overlooks the fact that the psychological subject here is not a man and is not even a group possessing a relatively unified and unchanging psychic structure, but, rather, is made up of different groups with different social and psychic interests. The different dogmas are an expression of just those conflicting interests, and the victory of a dogma is not the result of an inner psychic conflict analogous to that in an individual, but is the result, rather, of a historical development which, in consequence of quite different external circumstances (such as the stagnation and retrogression of the productive powers and of the social and political forces connected with them), leads to the victory of one movement and the defeat of another.

Reik views dogma as an expression of compulsive thinking, and ritual as an expression of collective compulsive action.

Certainly it is correct that in Christian dogma, as well as in many other dogmas, ambivalence toward the father plays a great role, but this in no way demonstrates that dogma fantasies are matters of compulsive thinking. We have tried to show precisely how the variations in the development of dogma, which at first suggest compulsive thinking, require, in fact, a different explanation. Dogma is to a large extent conditioned by realistic political and social motives. It serves as a sort of banner, and the recognition of the banner is the avowal of membership in a particular group. On this basis it is understandable that religions which are sufficiently consolidated by extra-religious elements (such as Judaism is by the ethnic element) are able to dispense almost completely with a system of dogmas in the Catholic sense.

But it is obvious that this organizing function of dogma is not its only function; and the present study has attempted to show what social significance is to be attributed to dogma by the fact that in fantasy it gratifies the demands of the people, and functions in place of real gratification. Given the fact that symbolic gratifications are condensed into the form of a dogma which the masses are required to believe on the authority of priests and rulers, it seems to us that dogma may be compared with a powerful suggestion by an authority, and experienced subjectively as reality because of the consensus among the believers. For the dogma to reach the unconscious, those contents which are not capable of being consciously perceived must be eliminated and presented in rationalized and acceptable forms.

7. CONCLUSION

Let us summarize what our study has shown concerning the meaning of the changes occurring in the evolution of the dogma of Christ.

The early Christian faith in the suffering man who became God had its central significance in the implied wish to overthrow the father-god or his earthly representatives. The figure of the suffering Jesus originated primarily from the need for identification on the part of the suffering masses, and it was only secondarily determined by the need for expiation for the crime of aggression against the father. The followers of this faith were men who, because of their fate, were imbued with hatred for their rulers and with hope for their own happiness. The change in the economic situation and in the social composition of the Christian community altered the psychic attitude of the believers. Dogma developed; the idea of a man becoming a god changes into the idea of a god becoming a man. No longer should the father be overthrown; it is not the rulers who are guilty but the suffering masses. Aggression is no longer directed against the rulers but against the persons of the sufferers themselves. The satisfaction lies in pardon and love, which the father offers his submissive sons, and simultaneously in the regal, fatherly position which the suffering Jesus assumes while remaining the representative of the suffering masses. Jesus eventually became God without overthrowing God because. He was always God. Behind this there lies a still deeper regression which finds expression in the Homoousian dogma: the fatherly God, whose pardon is to be obtained only through one's own suffering, is transformed into the mother full of grace who nourishes the child, shelters it in her womb, and thus provides pardon. Described psychologically, the change taking place here is the change from an attitude hostile to the father, to an attitude passively and masochistically docile, and finally to that of the infant loved by its mother. If this development took place in an individual, it would indicate a psychic illness. It takes place over a period of centuries, however, and affects not the entire psychic structure of individuals but only a segment common to all; it is an expression not of pathological disturbance but, rather, of adjustment to the given social situation. For the masses who retained a remnant of hope for the overthrow of the rulers, the early Christian fantasy was suitable and satisfying, as was Catholic dogma for the masses of the Middle Ages. The cause for the development lies in the change in the socio-economic situation or in the retrogression of productive forces and their social consequences. The ideologists of the dominant classes strengthened and accelerated this development by suggesting symbolic satisfactions to the masses, guiding their aggression into socially harmless channels.

Catholicism signified the disguised return to the religion of the Great Mother who had been defeated by Jahwe. Only Protestantism turned back to the father-god.[59] It stands at the beginning of a social epoch that permits an active attitude on the part of the masses in contrast to the passively infantile attitude of the Middle Ages.[60]

This essay was translated from the German by James Luther Adams

[59] Luther personally was characterized by his ambivalent attitude to the father; the partly loving, partly hostile encounter between him and the father-figures constituted the central point of his psychic situation.

[60] Cf. Frazer, *The Golden Bough*; and also the conception, related to ours, in A. J. Storfer, *Marias jungfräuliche Mutterschaft*, Berlin, 1913.

2

THE PRESENT HUMAN CONDITION

When the medieval world was destroyed, Western man seemed to be headed for the final fulfilment of his keenest dreams and visions. He freed himself from the authority of a totalitarian church, the weight of traditional thought, the geographical limitations of our only half-discovered globe. He built a new science which eventually has led to the release of hitherto unheard-of productive powers and to the complete transformation of the material world. He created political systems which seem to guarantee the free and productive development of the individual; he reduced work time to such an extent that Western man is free to enjoy hours of leisure to an extent his forefathers had hardly dreamed of.

Yet where are we today?

The danger of an all-destructive war hangs over humanity, a danger which is by no means overcome by the hesitant attempts of governments to avoid it. But even if man's political representatives have enough sanity left to avoid a war, man's condition is far from the fulfilment of the hopes of the sixteenth, seventeenth, and eighteenth centuries.

Man's character has been moulded by the demands of the world he has built with his own hands. In the eighteenth and nineteenth centuries, the social character of the middle class showed strong exploitative and hoarding traits. This character was determined by the desire to exploit others and to save one's own earnings to make further profit from them. In the twentieth century, man's character orientation shows considerable passivity and an identification with the values of the market. Contemporary man is certainly passive in most of his leisure time. He is the eternal consumer; he "takes in" drink, food, cigarettes, lectures, sights, books, movies; all are consumed, swallowed. The world is one great object for his appetite, a big bottle, a big apple, a big breast. Man has become the suckler, the eternally expectant—and the eternally disappointed.

In so far as modern man is not the consumer, he is the trader. Our economic system is centred in the function of the market as determining the value of all commodities and as the regulator of each one's share in the social product. Neither force nor tradition, as in previous periods of history, nor fraud nor trickery govern man's economic activities. He is free to produce and to sell; market day is judgment day for the success of his efforts. Not only commodities are offered and sold on the market; labour has become a commodity sold on the labour market under the same conditions of fair competition. But the market system has reached out further than the economic sphere of commodities and labour. Man has transformed *himself* into a commodity, and experiences his life as capital to be invested profitably; if he succeeds in this he is "successful" and his life has meaning; if not, "he is a failure". His "value" lies in his saleability, not in his human qualities of love and reason nor in his artistic capacities. Hence his sense of his own value depends on extraneous factors—his success, the judgment of others. Hence he is dependent on these others, and his security lies in conformity, in never being more than two feet away from the herd.

However, it is not only the market that determines modern man's character. Another factor, closely related to the market function, is the mode of industrial production. Enterprises become bigger and bigger; the number of people employed by these enterprises as workers or clerks grows incessantly: ownership is separated from management, and the industrial giants are governed by a professional bureaucracy interested mainly in the smooth functioning and in the expansion of their enterprise rather than in the personal greed for profit *per se*.

What kind of man, then, does our society need in order to function smoothly? It needs men who co-operate easily in large groups, who want to consume more and more, and whose tastes are standardized and can be easily influenced and anticipated. It needs men who feel free and independent, not subject to any authority or principle or conscience, yet willing to be commanded, to do what is expected, to fit into the social machine without friction; men who can be guided without force, led without leaders, be prompted without an aim, except the aim to be on the move, to function, to go ahead. This kind of man, modern industrialism has succeeded in producing; he is the automaton, the alienated man. He is alienated in the sense that his actions and his own forces have become estranged from him; they stand above him and against him, and rule him rather than being ruled by him. His life forces have shed themselves into things and institutions; and these things and institutions have become idols. They are experienced not as the result of man's own efforts but as something apart from him, which he worships and to which he submits. Alienated man bows down before the work of his own hands. His idols represent his own life forces in an alienated form. Man experiences himself not as the active bearer of his own forces and riches but as an impoverished "thing", dependent on other things outside of himself, into which he has projected his living substance.

Man's social feelings are projected into the state. As a citizen he is willing even to give his life for his fellow men; as a *private* individual he is governed by egotistical concern with himself. Because he has made the state the embodiment of his own social feelings, he worships it and its symbols. He projects his sense of power, wisdom, and courage into his leaders, and he worships these leaders as his idols. As a worker, clerk, or manager, modern man is alienated from his work. The worker has become an economic atom that dances to the tune of automatized management. He has no part in planning the work process, no part in its outcome; he is seldom in touch with the whole product. The manager, on the other hand, is in touch with the whole product, but he is alienated from it as something concrete—useful. His aim is to employ profitably the capital invested by others; the commodity is merely the embodiment of capital, not something which, as a concrete entity, matters to him. The manager has become a bureaucrat who handles things, figures, and human beings as mere objects of his activity. Their manipulation is called concern with human relations whereas the manager deals with the most inhuman relations, between automatons that have become abstractions.

Our consumption is equally alienated. It is determined by advertising slogans rather than by our real needs, by our palates, our eyes, or our ears.

The meaninglessness and alienation of work result in a longing for complete laziness. Man hates his working life because it makes him feel a prisoner and a fraud. His ideal becomes absolute laziness—in which he does not have to make a move, where everything proceeds according to the Kodak slogan "You press the button; we do the rest". This tendency is reinforced by the type of consumption necessary for the expansion of the inner market, leading to a principle which Huxley has very succinctly expressed in his *Brave New World*. One of the slogans which everyone is conditioned with from childhood is: "Never put off till tomorrow the fun you can have today." If I do not postpone the satisfaction of my wish (and I am conditioned only to wish for what I can get), I have no conflicts, no doubts; no decision has to be made; I am never alone with myself because I am always busy—either working or having fun. I have no need to be aware of myself as myself because I am constantly absorbed with consuming. I am a system of desire and satisfactions; I have to work in order to fulfil my desires—and these very desires are constantly stimulated and directed by the economic machine.

We claim that we pursue the aims of the Judaeo-Christian tradition: the love of God and of our neighbour. We are even told that we are going through a period of a promising religious renaissance. Nothing could be further from the truth. We use symbols belonging to a genuinely religious tradition and transform them into formulas serving the purpose of alienated man. Religion has become an empty shell; it has been transformed into a self-help device for increasing one's own powers for success. God becomes a partner in business. *The Power of Positive Thinking* is the successor of *How to Make Friends and Influence People*.

Love of man is a rare phenomenon too. Automatons do not love; alienated men do not care. What is praised by love experts and marriage counsellors is a team relationship between two people who manipulate each other with the right techniques and whose love is essentially a haven from an otherwise unbearable aloneness, an egotism *à deux*.

What, then, can be expected from the future? If we ignore those thoughts which are only the products of our wishes, we have to admit, I am afraid, that the most likely possibility is still that the discrepancy between technical intelligence and reason will lead the world into an atomic war. The most likely outcome of such a war is the destruction of industrial civilization and the regression of the world to a primitive agrarian level. Or, if the destruction should not prove to be as thorough as many specialists in the field believe, the result will be the necessity for the victor to organize and dominate the whole world. This could happen only in a centralized state based on force, and it would make little difference whether Moscow or Washington were the seat of government.

Unfortunately, even the avoidance of war does not promise a bright future. In the development of both capitalism and communism, as we visualize them in the next fifty or a hundred years, the processes that encourage human alienation will continue. Both systems are developed into managerial societies, their inhabitants well fed, well clad, having their wishes satisfied, and not having wishes which cannot be satisfied. Men are increasingly automatons, who follow without force, who are guided without leaders, who make machines which act like men and produce men who act like machines; their reason deteriorates while their intelligence rises, thus creating the dangerous situation of equipping man with the greatest material power without the wisdom to use it.

In spite of increasing production and comfort, man loses more and more the sense of self, feels that his life is meaningless, even though such a feeling is largely unconscious. In the nineteenth century the problem was that *God is dead*; in the twentieth century the problem is that *man is dead*. In the nineteenth century inhumanity meant cruelty; in the twentieth century it means schizoid self-alienation. The danger of the past was that men became slaves. The danger of the future is that men may become robots. True enough, robots do not rebel. But given man's nature, robots cannot live and remain sane; they become "Golems"; they will destroy their world and themselves because they will be able to stand no longer the boredom of a meaningless life.

What is the alternative to war and robotism? Most fundamentally, perhaps, the answer could be given by reversing Emerson's phrase "Things are in the saddle and ride mankind" and saying, "Put mankind in the saddle so that they ride things." This is another way of saying that man must overcome the alienation which makes him an impotent and irrational worshipper of idols. This means, in the psychological sphere, that he must overcome the market-oriented and passive attitudes which dominate him now, and choose a mature, and productive path. He must acquire again a sense of self; he must be capable of loving and of making his work a meaningful and concrete activity. He must emerge from a materialistic orientation and arrive at a level where spiritual values—love, truth, and justice—truly become of ultimate concern to him. But any attempt to change only one section of life, the human or the spiritual, is doomed to failure. In fact, progress that takes place in only one sphere is destructive of progress in all spheres. The Gospel concerned only with spiritual salvation led to the establishment of the Roman Catholic Church; the French Revolution, with its concern exclusively with political reform, led to Robespierre and Napoleon; socialism, inasmuch as it was concerned only with economic change, led to Stalinism.

Applying the principle of simultaneous change to all spheres of life, we must think of the economic and political changes necessary in order to overcome the psychological fact of alienation. We must retain the technological advances of large-scale machine production and automation. But we must decentralize work and the state so as to give them *human proportions*, and must permit centralization only to the point necessary for the requirements of industry. In the economic sphere, we need industrial democracy, a democratic socialism characterized by the co-management of all who work in an enterprise, in order to permit their active and responsible participation. The new forms for such participation can be found. In the political sphere, effective democracy can be established by creating thousands of small face-to-face groups which are well informed, which discuss, and whose decisions are integrated in a new "lower house". A cultural renaissance must combine work education for the young, adult education, and a new system of popular art and secular ritual throughout the whole nation.

Just as primitive man was helpless before the natural forces, so modern man is helpless before the social and economic forces he himself has created. He worships the works of his own hands, bowing to the new idols, yet swearing by the God who commanded him to destroy all idols. Man can protect himself from the consequences of his own madness only by creating a sane society which conforms to the needs of man, needs which are rooted in the very conditions of his existence. A society in which man relates to man lovingly, in which he is rooted in bonds of brotherliness and solidarity rather than in the ties of blood and soil; a society which gives him the possibility of transcending nature by creating rather than by destroying, in which everyone gains a sense of self by experiencing himself as the subject of his powers rather than by conformity, in which a system of orientation and devotion exists without requiring him to distort reality and to worship idols.

Building such a society means taking the next step; it means the end of "humanoid" history, the phase in which man has not yet become fully human. It does not mean the "end of days", the "completion", the state of perfect harmony in which no conflicts or problems confront man. On the contrary, it is man's fate that his existence is beset by contradictions which he is impelled to solve without ever solving them. When he has overcome the primitive state of human sacrifice, be it in the ritualistic form of the human sacrifices of the Aztecs or in the secular form of war, when he has been able to regulate his relationship with nature reasonably instead of blindly, when things have truly become his servants rather than his idols, he will be confronted with the truly human conflicts and problems; he will have to be adventuresome, courageous, imaginative, capable of suffering and of joy, but his powers will be in the service of life, not in the service of death. The new phase of human history, if it comes to pass, will be a new beginning, not an end.

3

SEX AND CHARACTER

The thesis that between the two sexes there are innate differences which necessarily result in basic differences in character and fate is a very old one. The Old Testament makes it woman's peculiarity and curse that her "desire shall be to thy husband and he shall rule over thee", and man's that he shall have to work in sweat and sorrow. But even the biblical report contains virtually the opposite thesis: man was created in God's likeness, and only as punishment for man's and woman's original disobedience—they were treated as equals with regard to their moral responsibility—were they cursed with mutual conflict and eternal difference. Both these views, that of their basic difference and that of their basic identity, have been repeated through the centuries—one age or one philosophical school emphasizing the one; another, the opposite thesis.

The problem assumed increased significance in the philosophical and political discussions of the eighteenth and nineteenth centuries. Representatives of the Enlightenment philosophy took the position that there were no innate differences between the sexes (*l'âme n'a pas de sexe*); that whatever differences would be observed were conditioned by differences in education, were—as would be said today—cultural differences. Romantic philosophers of the early nineteenth century, on the other hand, stressed the very opposite point. They analyzed the characterological differences between men and women, and said that the fundamental differences were the result of innate biological and physiological differences. Their contention was that these differences in character would exist in any conceivable culture.

Regardless of the merits of the respective arguments—and the analysis of the Romantics was often profound—they both had a political implication. The philosophers of the Enlightenment, especially the French, wanted to make a point for the social and, to some extent, political equality of men and women. They emphasized the lack of innate differences as an argument for their case. The Romantics, who were political reactionaries, used their analysis of the essence (*Wesen*) of man's nature as a proof for the necessity of political and social inequality. Although they attributed very admirable qualities to "the woman", they insisted that her characteristics made her unfit to participate in social and political life on an equal footing with men.

The political struggle for woman's equality did not end in the nineteenth century, nor did the theoretical discussion on the innate versus the cultural character of their differences. In modern psychology Freud became the most outspoken representative of the Romantics' cause. Whereas the argument of the latter had been couched in philosophical language, Freud's was based on the scientific observation of patients in the psychoanalytic procedure. He assumed that the anatomical difference between the sexes was the cause for unalterable characterological differences. "Anatomy is her fate," he says of the woman, paraphrasing a sentence of Napoleon's. His contention was that the little girl, when she discovers the fact that she lacks the male genital organ, is profoundly shocked and impressed by this discovery; that she feels something she ought to have is lacking; that she envies men for having what fate has denied her; that in the normal course of development she will try to overcome her feeling of inferiority and envy by substituting other things for the male genital organ: husband, children, or possessions. In the case of neurotic development she does not succeed in making such satisfactory substitutions. She remains envious of all men, does not give up her wish to be a man, becomes homosexual or hates men, or seeks certain culturally permitted compensations. Even in the case of normal development, the tragic quality of woman's fate never quite disappears; she is cursed with a wish to obtain something which remains unattainable throughout her life.

Although orthodox psychoanalysts retained this theory of Freud as one of the cornerstones of their psychological system, another group of culturally oriented psychoanalysts disputed Freud's findings. They showed the fallacies, both clinical and theoretical, in Freud's reasoning by pointing to the cultural and personal experiences of women in modern society that caused the characterological results which he had explained on biological grounds. The views of this group of psychoanalysts found confirmation in the findings of the anthropologists.

Nevertheless, there exists a certain danger that some followers of those progressive anthropological and psychoanalytic theories will lean over backward and deny completely that biological differences have any effect in moulding the character structure. They may be prompted to do so by the same motivation that was found in the representatives of the French Enlightenment. Since the emphasis on innate differences is used as an argument by the enemies of woman's equality, it may seem necessary to prove that there were none but cultural causes for any differences that may be empirically observed.

It is important to recognize that a significant philosophical question is involved in this whole controversy. The tendency to deny any characterological differences between the sexes may be prompted by the implicit acceptance of one of the premises of anti-equalitarian philosophy: in order to demand equality one has to prove that there are no characterological differences between the sexes except those caused directly by existing social conditions. The whole discussion is particularly involved because one group is speaking of *differences*, whereas the reactionaries really mean *deficiencies*—and, more specifically, those deficiencies which make it impossible for full equality to be shared with the majority group. Thus women's alleged limited intelligence and lack of faculties for organization and for abstraction or critical judgment were held to preclude their full equality with men. One school of thought said they possessed intuition, love, and so on, but that these qualities did not seem to make them more fit for the task of modern society. The same is often said about minorities such as the Negroes and the Jews. Thus the psychologist or anthropologist was put in a position where he had to disprove that among sex or racial groups there were any fundamental differences which had anything to do with their ability to share full equality. In this position the liberal thinker was inclined to minimize the existence of any distinctions.

Although the liberals proved that differences justifying political, economic, and social inequality do not exist, they allowed themselves to be pushed into a strategically unfavourable defensive position. Establishing the fact that there are no *socially damaging* differences does not require one to hold that that there are no differences at all. Properly then, the question is: What use is made of the existing or alleged differences, and what political purposes do they serve? Even granted that women show certain characterological differences from men, what does it mean?

It is the thesis of this paper that certain biological differences result in characterological differences; that such differences are blended with those which are directly produced by social factors; that the latter are much stronger in their effect and can either increase, eliminate, or reverse biologically rooted differences; and that eventually, characterological differences between the sexes, inasmuch as they are not directly determined by culture, never constitute differences in value. In other words, the character typical of men and women in Western culture is determined by their respective social roles, but there is a colouring of character which is rooted in sex differences. This colouring is insignificant in comparison with the socially rooted differences, but it must not be neglected.

The implicit assumption underlying much reactionary thinking is that equality presupposes an absence of differences between persons or social groups. Since such differences obviously exist with regard to practically everything that matters in life, their conclusion is that there can be no equality. When, conversely, the liberals are moved to deny the fact that there are great differences in mental and physical gifts and favourable or unfavourable accidental personality conditions, they only help their adversaries to appear right in the eyes of the common man. The concept of equality as it has developed in Judaeo-Christian and in modern progressive tradition means that all men are equal in such basic human capacities as those making for the enjoyment of freedom and happiness. It means, furthermore, that as a political consequence of this basic equality, no man shall be made the means to the ends of another man, no group the means to the ends of another group. Each man is a universe for himself, and is only his own purpose. His goal is the realization of his being, including those very peculiarities which are characteristic of him and make him different from others. Thus, equality is the basis for the full development of differences, and it results in the development of individuality.

Although there are a number of biological differences which might well be examined with regard to their relevance to character differences between men and women, this chapter will deal mainly with only one. Our purpose here is not so much to examine the whole problem of character differences between the sexes as to illustrate the general thesis. We shall mainly concern ourselves with the respective roles of men and women in sexual intercourse and shall undertake to show that this difference results in certain characterological differences—differences which only colour the main differences that arise from the difference in their social roles.

In order to function sexually, the man must have an erection and must be able to retain it during intercourse until he has had an orgasm; in order to satisfy the woman, he must be able to retain the erection for a sufficiently long time so that she may have an orgasm. This means that in order to satisfy the woman sexually the man has to *demonstrate* that he has the ability to have and maintain an erection. The woman, on the other hand, in order to satisfy the man sexually needs to demonstrate nothing. To be sure, her excitement may enhance the man's pleasure. Certain accompanying physical changes in her sexual organs may make intercourse easier for him. Since only purely sexual reactions are to be considered—not the subtle psychic reactions of differentiated personalities—the fact remains that the man needs to have an erection to satisfy the woman; the woman needs to have nothing but a certain amount of willingness to satisfy the man. In speaking of willingness it is important to note that the woman's availability for the sexual satisfaction of the man is dependent on her will; it is a conscious decision she can make at any time she pleases. The man's availability, however, is by no means simply a function of his will. As a matter of fact, he may have sexual desire and an erection against his will, and he may be impotent despite an ardent wish to the contrary. Furthermore, on the man's side, an inability to function is a fact which cannot be concealed. The woman's lack of either total or partial response, *her* "failure", though often recognizable to the man, is by no means similarly obvious; it permits a great deal of deception. If the woman consents with her will, the man can be sure of being satisfied whenever he desires her. But the situation of the woman is entirely different; the most ardent sexual desire on her side will not lead to satisfaction unless the man is sufficiently desirous of her to have an erection. And even during the sexual act the woman must depend for her full satisfaction on the man's ability to carry her to orgasm. Thus, to satisfy the partner the man has to prove something; the woman does not.

From this difference in their respective sexual roles something else follows—the difference in their specific anxieties connected with the sexual function. The anxiety is located at the very spot where the man's and the woman's position are vulnerable. The man's position is vulnerable in so far as he has to prove something, that is, in so far as he can potentially fail. To him, intercourse has always the colouring of a test, of an examination. His specific anxiety is that of *failing*. Fear of castration is the extreme case—fear of becoming organically and therefore permanently unable to perform. The woman's vulnerability, on the other hand, lies in her dependency on the man; the element of insecurity connected with her sexual function lies not in failing but in being "left alone", in being frustrated, in not having complete control over the process which leads to sexual satisfaction. It is not surprising, then, that the anxieties of men and women refer to different spheres—the man's concerning his ego, his prestige, his value in the eyes of the woman; the woman's concerning her sexual pleasure and satisfaction.[1]

The reader may now ask: Are not these anxieties characteristic only of neurotic personalities? Is not the normal man sure of his potency? Is not the normal woman sure of her partner? Is one not concerned here with the highly nervous and sexually

[1] A similar distinction, referring to differences in the sexual fears of children only, has been made by Karen Horney, "Die Angst vor der Frau", *Zeitschr. f. Psychoanal.*, 13 (1932), pp. 1–18.

insecure modern man? Are not the "cave man" and the "cave woman", with their "primitive" and unspoiled sexuality, free from such doubts and anxieties?

At first glance this might seem to be the case. The man who is constantly worried about his potency represents a certain type of neurotic personality, as does the woman who is constantly afraid of remaining unsatisfied or who suffers from her dependency. Here, as is so often the case, the difference between the "neurotic" and the "normal" is one of degree and of awareness rather than one of essential quality. What appears as a conscious and continuous anxiety in the neurotic person is a relatively unnoticed and quantitatively slight anxiety in the so-called normal man. The same is true in the case of women. Furthermore, in normal individuals, anxieties are not aroused by certain incidents which are sure to cause manifest anxiety in the neurotic person. The normal man does not doubt his potency. The normal woman is not afraid of being sexually frustrated by the man she has chosen for a sexual partner. To choose the very man whom she can have "faith" in sexually is an essential part of her healthy sexual instinct. But this in no way alters the fact that *potentially* the man can fail, but never the woman. The woman is dependent on the man's desire, not the man on hers.

There is still another element which is significant in determining the presence of anxieties and of *different* anxieties in the normal man and woman.

The difference between the sexes is the basis for the earliest and most elementary division of mankind into separate groups. Man and woman need each other, for the maintenance of the race and of the family, as well as for the satisfaction of their sexual desires. But in any situation in which two different groups need each other, there will be elements not only of harmony, co-operation, and mutual satisfaction but also of struggle and disharmony.

The sexual relationship between the sexes could scarcely be

free from potential antagonism and hostility. Men and women have, along with the capacity to love each other, a similar capacity to hate. In any man-woman relationship the element of antagonism is a potentiality, and from this very potentiality the element of anxiety must at times arise. The beloved one may turn into an enemy, and then the vulnerable points of man and woman respectively are threatened.

The kind of threat and anxiety, however, is different for men than for women. If the man's main anxiety is that of failing in or not performing the expected task, the drive designed to protect him from this anxiety is the wish for prestige. The man is deeply pervaded by a craving to prove constantly to himself, to the woman he loves, to all other women, and to all other men that he lives up to any expectation of him. He seeks reassurance against the fear of sexual failing by competing in all other spheres of life in which will-power, physical strength, and intelligence are useful in assuring success. Closely linked with this craving for prestige is his competitive attitude toward other men. Being afraid of possible failure, he tends to prove that he is better than any other man. The Don Juan does so directly in the sexual realm; the average man indirectly—by killing more enemies, hunting more deer, making more money, or being more successful in other ways than his male competitors.

The modern social and economic system is based on the principles of competition and success; ideologies praise its value, and by these and other circumstances the craving for prestige and competitiveness is firmly implanted in the average human being living within Western culture. Even if there were no difference in the respective sexual roles, these cravings would exist in men and women on the strength of social factors. The impact of these social sources is so great that it might seem doubtful whether, in quantitative terms, there is any marked predominance of the craving for prestige in men as a result of the sexual factors which this paper discusses. The matter of first importance is not the degree to which competitiveness is increased by the sexual sources but rather the need that recognition be given to the presence of any factor other than the ones which make for competitiveness.

The masculine striving for prestige throws some light on the specific quality of male vanity. It is generally said that women are vainer than men. Although the reverse may be true, what matters is not the difference in *quantity* but in the *nature* of the vanity. The essential feature of man's vanity is to show off, to demonstrate what a good "performer" he is. He acts as if he lived in an unending examination dream. He is eager to assert that he is not afraid of failing. This vanity seems to colour all of man's activity. There is probably no achievement of men, from making love to the most courageous acts in fighting or thinking, which is not coloured to some degree by this typical male vanity.

Another aspect of man's craving for prestige is his sensitivity toward ridicule, particularly toward ridicule from women. Even a coward may become something of a hero under the fear of being ridiculed by women, and the man's fear of losing his life may be less great than his fear of ridicule. As a matter of fact, this is typical in the pattern of male heroism, which is no greater than the heroism of which women are capable, but different because it is coloured by the male kind of vanity.

Another result of man's precarious position toward woman and his fear of her ridicule is his potential hatred for her. This hatred contributes to a striving which has also a defensive function: to dominate the woman, to have power over her, to make her feel weak and inferior. If he succeeds in this, he need not be afraid of her. If she is afraid of him—afraid of being killed, beaten, or starved—she cannot ridicule him. Power over a person is dependent neither on one's intensity of passion nor on the functioning of one's sexual and emotional productiveness. Power depends on factors which can be so securely maintained that no doubt of incompetency need ever arise. Incidentally, the promise of power over woman is the comfort which the patriarchally biased biblical myth holds out to the man even while God curses him.

To return to the problem of vanity, we have stated that woman's vanity differs qualitatively from that of the man. The man's vanity is to show what he can *do*, to prove that he never fails; the woman's vanity is essentially continued by the need to attract, and the need to prove to herself that she can attract. To be sure, the man needs to attract a woman sexually in order to win her. This holds true especially in a culture where differentiated tastes and feelings are involved in sexual attraction. But there are other ways by which a man can gain a woman and induce her to be his sexual partner: sheer physical power or, more significantly, social power and wealth. His opportunities for sexual satisfaction do not depend solely on his sexual attractiveness. Her sexual satisfaction depends entirely on her attractiveness. Neither force nor promises can make a man sexually potent. The woman's attempt to be attractive is necessitated by her sexual role, and her vanity or concern with her attractiveness results from this.

The woman's fear of dependency, of frustration, of a role which forces her to wait, frequently leads to a wish which Freud has stressed heavily: the wish to have the male genital organ.[2] The root for this wish, however, is not that the woman primarily feels she lacks something, that she is inferior to the man for want of the penis. Although in many instances there are other reasons, the wish of the woman to have a penis often springs from her wish not to be dependent, not to be restricted in her activity, not to be exposed to the danger of frustration. Just as the man's wish to be a woman may result from his desire to be rid of the burden of the *test*, the woman's wish to have a penis may result from her

[2] Cf. Clara Thompson, "What Is Penic Envy?" and the discussion which follows by Janet Rioch, *Proceedings of the Association for the Advancement of Psychoanalysis*, Boston Meetings, 1942.

desire to overcome her dependence. Also, under special circumstances but not infrequently, not only does the penis serve as a symbol of independence but, in the service of sadistic-aggressive tendencies, it also symbolizes a weapon with which to hurt men or other women.[3]

If the man's main weapon against the woman is his physical and social power over her, then her main weapon is her ability to ridicule him. The most radical way in which to ridicule him is to make him impotent. There are many ways, including crude and subtle ones, in which the woman does this. They range from the expressed or implied expectation of his failure, to frigidity and the sort of vaginal spasm which makes intercourse physically impossible. The wish to castrate the man does not seem to play the all-important role that Freud ascribes to it. To be sure, castration is one way to render the man impotent, and this often appears when destructive and sadistic tendencies are marked. But the main aim of woman's hostility does seem to be not physical but functional damage, to interfere with the man's ability to perform. Man's specific hostility is to *overpower* by physical force, political or economic power; woman's to *undermine*, by ridicule and contempt.

Women can bear children; men cannot. Characteristically, from his patriarchal viewpoint, Freud assumed that the woman is envious of the male organ, but he scarcely noted the possibility that men are envious of women's ability to bear children. This one-sided view not only comes from the masculine premise that men are superior to women, but also results from the attitude of a highly technical-industrial civilization in which natural productiveness is not very highly valued. Nevertheless, if one considers earlier periods of human history, when life

[3] In female homosexuality a combination of the tendency to be active, in contrast to the "waiting" dependent role, along with definitely destructive tendencies, often seems to be a significant part of the picture.

depended essentially on the productivity of nature and not on technical productivity, the fact that women shared this gift with the soil and with female animals must have been exceedingly impressive. Man is sterile, if only the purely naturalistic realm is considered. In a culture in which the main emphasis was on natural productivity, one would assume that the man felt inferior to the woman especially when his role in the production of the child was not clearly understood. It is safe to assume that man admired woman for this capacity which he lacked, that he was awed by her and envious of her. He could not produce; he could only kill animals so that he could eat them, or kill enemies so that he could be safe or acquire their strength in some magical way.

Without discussing the place of these factors in purely agrarian communities, we shall touch briefly on the effects of some important historical changes. One of the most significant of these effects was the increasing application of the technical mode of production. More and more the mind was used to improve and increase the various means of living which originally were dependent on nature's gifts alone. Although women originally had a gift which made them superior to men and the latter originally compensated for this lack by using their skill for destruction, men later came to use their intellect as the basis for technical productivity. In its early stages this was closely linked with magic; later on, man by the power of his thought produced material things; his capacity for technical production has by now outstripped the reliance on natural production.

Rather than develop this topic at this point, we shall merely refer to the writings of Bachofen, Morgan, and Briffault, who have gathered and brilliantly analyzed anthropological material which, though it may not prove their theses, strongly suggests that in several phases of early history, certain cultures existed in which social organization was centred around the mother and in which mother-goddesses, identified with the productivity of nature, were the centre of man's religious ideas.[4]

One illustration will suffice. The Babylonian myth of creation starts with the existence of a mother-goddess – Tiamat – who rules over the universe. Her rule, however, is threatened by her male sons, who are planning to rebel and overthrow her. They seek as a leader for this fight somebody who can match her strength. Eventually they agree on Marduk, but, before definitely choosing him, they require him to undergo a test. What is the test? A coat is brought to him. He must "with the power of his mouth" make the coat disappear and then make it reappear again with a word. The chosen leader by a word destroys the coat and by a word re-creates it. His leadership is confirmed. He defeats the mother-goddess and from her body creates heaven and earth.

What is the meaning of this test? If the male god is to match the strength of the goddess, he must have the one quality which makes her superior—the power to create. The test is to prove that he has this power, as well as the characteristically masculine power to destroy, the way in which man traditionally changed nature. He first destroys, then re-creates, a material object; but he does this with his word and not, like the woman, with her womb. Natural productivity is replaced by the magic of thought and word processes.

The biblical creation myth starts where the Babylonian myth ends. Almost all traces of the supremacy of a female goddess have now been eliminated. The creation starts with God's magic, the magic of creation by word. The theme of male creation is repeated; contrary to fact, man is not born of woman, but

[4] See also Frieda Fromm-Reichmann, "Notes on the Mother Role in the Family Group". *Bulletin of the Menninger Clinic*, 4 (1940), pp. 132–48.

woman is made from man.[5] The biblical myth is a song of triumph over defeated woman; it denies that women bear men, and reverses the natural relations. In God's curse the supremacy of men is again upheld. The childbearing function of women is recognized, but it is to be painful. Man is destined to work, that is to say, to produce; thus he replaces the original productivity of the woman, even if this, too, is to be done in sweat and sorrow.

We have dealt at some length with the phenomenon of matriarchal remnants in the history of religion to illustrate one point which matters in the present context—the fact that the woman has the capacity of natural productiveness which the man lacks; that the man on this level is sterile. In certain periods of history this superiority of woman was consciously felt; later on, all the emphasis was on the magical and technical productivity of man. Nevertheless, it seems that unconsciously, even today, this difference has not entirely lost its meaning; somewhere in the man exists an awe of the woman for this capacity which he lacks. He is envious of it and fearful of it. Somewhere in his character is the need for a constant compensatory effort for his lack; somewhere in the woman, a feeling of superiority over him for his "sterility".

Thus far, we have dealt with certain characterological differences between men and women which have resulted from their sexual differences. Is this to be taken to mean that traits like over-dependence, on the one hand, and craving for prestige and competitiveness, on the other, are essentially caused by the sex differences? Are "a" woman and "a" man to be expected to exhibit these traits, so that if they have the traits characteristic of the other sex, this fact is to be explained by the presence of a homosexual component?

[5] Compare the Greek myth of Athena being born from the head of her father Zeus and the interpretation of this myth as well as the remnant of matriarchal religion in Greek mythology by Bachofen and Otto.

No conclusions of the kind follow. The sexual difference colours the personality of the average man and woman. This colouring may be compared to the key or the mode in which a melody is written, not to the melody itself. Furthermore, it refers only to the average man and woman respectively, and varies with every person.

These "natural" differences are blended with differences brought about by the specific culture in which people live. For instance, in our present-day culture, the craving for prestige and competitive success to be found in men has to do much less with sexual roles than with social roles. Society is organized in a way which necessarily produces these strivings, regardless of whether or not they have had roots in specific masculine or feminine peculiarities. The craving for prestige, as it has been found in modern man since the end of the Middle Ages, is conditioned chiefly by the social and economic system, not by his sexual role; the same is true of the dependency of women. What happens is that cultural patterns and social forms can create characterological trends which run parallel to identical tendencies rooted in entirely different sources, such as sexual differences. If that is the case, the two parallel trends are blended into one, and it seems as if their sources were identical.

The cravings for prestige and dependency respectively, inasmuch as they are products of culture, determine the whole personality. The individual personality is thus reduced to one segment of the whole gamut of human potentialities. But the characterological differences, inasmuch as they are rooted in natural differences, are not of this kind. The reason for this may be found in the fact that deeper than the *difference* between the sexes is their *equality*, the fact that men and women are first of all human beings sharing the same potentialities, the same desires, and the same fears. Whatever is different in them on account of natural differences does not make *them* different. It provides their personalities, which are fundamentally alike, with slight differences in the emphasis of one or another trend, an emphasis which appears empirically as a colouring. These differences which are rooted in sexual differences would seem to afford no basis for casting men and women in different roles in any given society.

It is apparent today that, whatever differences exist between the sexes, they are relatively insignificant in comparison with the characterological differences that are found between persons of the same sex. The sexual differences do not influence the capacity to do work of any kind. Certain highly differentiated achievements may be coloured in their quality by sexual characteristics—one sex may be somewhat more gifted for a certain kind of work than is the other—but such is the case if extraverts are compared with introverts, or pyknic with asthenic types. It would be a fatal misunderstanding to think of social, economic, and political differentiation according to such characteristics.

Again, in comparison with the general social influences which shape the masculine or feminine patterns, it is clear that the individual and, from a social standpoint, accidental experiences of any person are highly significant. These personal experiences in their turn blend themselves with the cultural patterns, mostly reinforcing but sometimes reducing their effects. The influence of the social and personal factors must be assumed to exceed in strength that of the "natural" ones which have been discussed here.

It is a sad commentary on the times that one feels it necessary to emphasize that the differences due to the male or female role do not lend themselves to any judgment of value from a social or a moral point of view. In and of themselves they are neither good nor bad, neither desirable nor unfortunate. The same trait will appear as a positive feature in one personality when certain conditions are present, and as a negative feature in another personality when other conditions are present. Thus the negative forms in which man's fear of failure and his need for prestige can appear are obvious: vanity, lack of seriousness, unreliability, and boastfulness. But it seems no less obvious that the very same trait can result in very positive character traits: initiative, activity, and courage. The same holds true with regard to the female characteristics as described above. The woman's peculiar characteristics can, and often do, result in her inability to "stand on her own feet" practically, emotionally, and intellectually; but, given other conditions, she becomes the source of patience, reliability, intensity of love, and of erotic charm.

The positive or negative outcome of the one or the other characteristic depends on the character structure as a whole of the person with whom one is dealing. Such personality factors making for a positive or a negative outcome are, for instance, anxiety versus self-reliance or destructiveness versus constructiveness, respectively. But it is not sufficient to single out one or two of the more isolated traits; only the *whole* of the character structure determines whether one of the masculine or feminine characteristics turns into a positive or a negative trait. This principle is the same as that which Klages has introduced in his system of graphology. Any single trait in the handwriting can have a positive *or* a negative meaning according to what he calls the *form-niveau* (the level of form) of the whole personality. If somebody's character can be called "orderly", it can mean one of two things: either it indicates something positive, namely, that he is not "sloppy", that he is capable of organizing his life; or it can mean something negative, namely, that he is pedantic, sterile, or without initiative. Obviously the trait *orderliness* is at the root of both the negative and the positive outcomes, but the outcome is determined by a number of other factors in the total personality; these, in their turn, depend on external conditions which make for growth or for a thwarting of life, respectively.

4

PSYCHOANALYSIS—SCIENCE OR PARTY LINE?

Freudian psychoanalysis as a therapy for the cure of neurosis and a scientific theory dealing with the nature of man is well known. What is somewhat less known is that it is also a "movement", with an international organization on strictly hierarchical lines, strict rules for belonging, and for many years guided by a secret committee consisting of Freud and six others. This movement has on occasion and in some of its representatives exhibited a fanaticism usually found only in religious and political bureaucracies.

The closest comparison, as far as another revolutionizing scientific theory is concerned, is Darwin's theory, whose impact on modern thought was, if anything, even more powerful than that of psychoanalysis. But is there a Darwinistic "movement" that determines who may call himself a "Darwinist", and is strictly organized and fanatically fighting for the purity of Darwin's doctrine?

I want first to demonstrate some of the more drastic and

unfortunate expressions of this "party line" spirit in connexion with Ernest Jones's recent biography of Freud. This seems to be indicated for two reasons: first, that Jones's party fanaticism led him to grotesque posthumous attacks on men who disagreed with Freud; and, second, that many reviewers of Jones's book have accepted his data without criticism or question.

Jones's "rewriting" of history introduces into science a method which thus far we have expected to find only in Stalinist "history". The Stalinists call those who defected and rebelled "traitors" and "spies" of capitalism. Dr. Jones does the same in psychiatric parlance by claiming that Rank and Ferenczi, the two men who were most closely linked with Freud and who later deviated from him in some respects, had been psychotic for many years. The implication is that only their insanity explains their crime of defecting from Freud and, in the case of Ferenczi, that his complaints about Freud's harsh and intolerant treatment of him are *ipso facto* evidence of psychosis.

First of all, it is noteworthy that for many years before there was any question of Rank's or Ferenczi's "disloyalty", there were within the secret Committee violent fights and jealousies between Abraham, Jones, and, to some extent, Eitingon on the one hand and Rank and Ferenczi on the other. Already in 1924, when Rank published his book on the birth trauma, which Freud received at that time with friendliness, Abraham, "encouraged on hearing that Freud was open to criticism", suspected Rank of following Jung's path of "treason".

Though Freud at first reacted with tolerance to Rank's new theories, later, probably under the influence of the intrigues and insinuations of the Jones faction and also because of Rank's unwillingness to modify his theoretical lines, Freud broke with Rank. At that time Freud spoke of Rank's neurosis as being responsible for some of his deviations; but only eighteen months before, Freud had said that in fifteen years "he had scarcely ever had the idea that Rank needed analysis".

However this may be, Freud speaks of *neurosis*, not of *psychosis*. Jones suggests that Freud repressed the knowledge that Rank suffered from "manic-depressive psychosis", a knowledge Freud is supposed to have had "years before". In view of Freud's own statement just mentioned, Jones's suggestion does not sound entirely convincing. (Also because the only reference to Freud's alleged knowledge is to a letter Freud wrote to Ferenczi in the same year, not years before.) A whole history is constructed to explain the existence of this alleged psychosis. Its foundations are laid in the five years after World War I, during which Rank worked very hard, and successfully, in directing the affairs of the psychoanalytical publishing house in Vienna. These five years, "in which Rank continued in this furious tempo, must have been a factor in his subsequent mental breakdown". For a psychiatrist, not to speak of a psychoanalyst, to explain a manic-depressive psychosis as being caused partly by overwork is quite unusual.

By 1923 "the evil spirit of dissension arose"; at that time Freud blamed Jones and Abraham for the disintegration of the Central Committee. But in the end Jones was to win out over his rivals. "It was only after the lapse of a few years that the true sources of the trouble became manifest: *namely, in the failing mental integration of Rank and Ferenczi*." This leads up to the crowning statement. The losers in the interfactional fight, Rank and Ferenczi, had carried the germ of a psychosis for many years, but these psychotic germs became manifest only when the two men disagreed with Freud. When they refused to appease Freud, the psychosis revealed itself! As Jones put it with refreshing frankness, Freud's hope,

> when founding the Committee, was that the six of us were suitably endowed for that purpose. It turned out, alas, that only four of us were. Two of the members, Rank and Ferenczi, were not able to hold out to the end. Rank in a dramatic fashion . . . and Ferenczi more gradually toward the end of his life

> developed psychotic manifestations that *revealed* themselves *in, among other ways, a turning away from Freud and his doctrines. The seeds of a destructive psychosis, invisible for so long, at last germinated.* [italics added]

If what Jones writes was true, it was indeed a most amazing oversight on Freud's part that not until the moment of manifest conflict did he see the psychotic development in two of his closest pupils and friends. Jones makes no attempt to give objective proof for his statement about Rank's alleged manic-depressive psychosis. We have only Jones's statement, that is, only the statement of a man who had been intriguing against Rank and suspecting him of disloyalty for many years in this fight within the court around Freud. On the other hand, there is plenty of evidence to the contrary. I quote only from a statement by Dr. Harry Bone, a psychoanalyst in New York who had known Rank since 1932 and was in frequent personal contact with him until his death. Dr. Bone states:

> In all the numerous times and all the quite various situations in which I had the opportunity to see him in action and in repose I sensed no indication either of psychosis or of any mental abnormality whatsoever.[1]

Rank at least made an open break with Freud, but Ferenczi never did so. It is all the more astonishing, therefore, that Ferenczi should also have been accused by Jones of betrayal. As in the case of Jung and Rank, the story of the betrayal is supposed to have begun with a fatal trip to America. When Ferenczi wanted to go to New York, some "intuitive foreboding, probably based on the unfortunate sequels of Jung's and Rank's similar visits", prompted Jones to advise him to decline. Nevertheless,

[1] Personal communication.

fully supported by Freud, Ferenczi left for the United States, and the "outcome was to justify my [Jones's] foreboding. Ferenczi was never the same man again after that visit, although it was another *four or five years until his mental depression became manifest to Freud*". [italics added]

In the next years, fantastic rivalries and intrigues between Jones and Ferenczi seem to have continued. Ferenczi suspected Jones of lying and of the ambition, based on financial motives, to unite the Anglo-Saxon nations under his, Jones's, sceptre. According to Jones, "Freud was thereby influenced unfavourably against me." But the anti-Ferenczi forces seem to have won in the end. Freud wrote Ferenczi in December 1929:

> You have without doubt withdrawn yourself outwardly from me in the past few years, but not so far, I hope, that a move toward creating a new oppositional analysis has to be expected from my Paladin and secret Grand Vizier!

What was the essence of the theoretical difference between Freud and Ferenczi? Ferenczi had been quite impressed by the importance of parental unkindness, and he believed that in order to be cured the patient needed more than "interpretations", that he needed the kind of motherly love that had been denied him when a child. Ferenczi changed his attitude to the patient from that of a detached observer to that of a participant, loving human being, and he was himself very enthusiastic about the therapeutic results of the new attitude. Freud seemed at first to have reacted with tolerance to this innovation. But his attitude changed, apparently because Ferenczi was not sufficiently ready to appease him, but perhaps also because the suspicions cast on Ferenczi by the Jones faction had their effect.

Ferenczi saw Freud for the last time in 1932, before the Congress in Wiesbaden. This visit was a truly tragic occasion. Freud summed up his final impressions of the man who had been his devoted follower and friend since the early years of the movement in a cable to Eitingon: "Ferenczi inaccessible, impression unsatisfactory." Ferenczi told Dr. Clara Thompson[2] of the visit immediately after it took place, in the train that brought them from Vienna to Germany. He said that the visit had been "terrible" and that Freud had told him that, though he might read his paper at the psychoanalytic congress in Wiesbaden, he should promise him not to publish it. Shortly thereafter, Ferenczi noticed the first symptoms of pernicious anaemia, the disease which caused his death the following year.

But some time before his last meeting with Freud, Ferenczi had told Mrs. Izette de Forest[3] how sad and hurt he had felt at the harsh and hostile way Freud had treated him.[4] This treatment of Ferenczi shows a remarkable intolerance. Yet Freud's inability to forgive a former friend who deviated from him is shown even more drastically in the contemptuous hate he expressed upon the death of Alfred Adler.

> For a Jew-boy out of a Viennese suburb a death in Aberdeen is an unheard-of career in itself, and a proof how far he had got on. The world really rewarded him richly for his service of contradicting psychoanalysis.

In the case of Ferenczi, to call this attitude "harsh" or "almost enmity", as Izette de Forest has done in *The Leaven of Love*, is a rather mild characterization. Jones, however, who denies that Freud had any traces of authoritarianism and intolerance, flatly asserts that there is no truth in any such story of hostility,

[2] A student and friend of Ferenczi's, now Director of the William Alanson White Institute of Psychiatry, Psychoanalysis, and Psychology in New York.
[3] A student and friend of Ferenczi, psychoanalyst and author of *The Leaven of Love*, which contains an excellent exposition of Ferenczi's new ideas on technique.
[4] Personal communication.

"although it is highly probable that Ferenczi himself, in his final *delusional state*, believed in and propagated elements of it".

Only a few weeks before his death, Ferenczi sent Freud congratulations on his birthday, but allegedly "the mental disturbance had been making rapid progress in the last few months". According to Jones (giving no source), Ferenczi related that one of his American patients had analyzed him and thus cured him of all his troubles, and that messages came from him to her across the Atlantic. Jones must admit, however, that Ferenczi had always been a staunch believer in telepathy, which rather destroys the "proof" of Ferenczi's madness. The only available "proof" is "the delusions about Freud's supposed hostility". Apparently Jones assumes that only a diseased mind can accuse Freud of authoritarianism and hostility.

Jones now brings the story of Ferenczi's alleged psychosis, the germs of which are supposed to have existed earlier, to a climax. When the disease attacked the spinal cord and the brain, this, according to Jones, undoubtedly was "exacerbated by his *latent* psychotic trends". In almost his last letter to Freud, after Hitler's coming to power, Ferenczi suggested to Freud that he go to England. Jones interprets this rather realistic advice as a sign "that there was some *method in his madness*". "Eventually, toward the end, came *violent paranoic and even homicidal outbursts*, which were followed by sudden death on May 24." Jones does not claim any firsthand knowledge, nor is any proof or evidence whatsoever offered of Ferenczi's psychosis nor of the "violent paranoic or even homicidal outbursts". In view of this, and of the following statements, Jones's assertions about Rank's and Ferenczi's psychosis must be judged untrue and open to the suspicion that they are the fabrications of wishful thinking, motivated by old personal jealousies and by the wish to spare Freud the criticism of having been unkind and harsh to men deeply devoted to him. (I do not mean to accuse Dr. Jones of conscious insincerity; that unconscious strivings can defeat conscious intentions is another matter, however, and exactly the subject matter of psychoanalysis.)

Jones did not see Ferenczi in the last year of his illness. But Dr. Clara Thompson, who was with Ferenczi from 1932 till the day of his death, states:

> . . . except for the symptoms of his physical illness, there was nothing psychotic in his reactions which I observed. I visited him regularly, and talked with him, and there was not a single incident, aside from memory difficulties, which would substantiate Jones's picture of Ferenczi's psychosis or homicidal mood.

Dr. Michael Balint, one of Ferenczi's most trusted disciples and executor of his literary estate, also disagrees with Dr. Jones's assertion. He writes:

> Despite this very serious neurological condition [in connexion with his pernicious anaemia] his mind remained clear till the end and I can vouch for that from personal experience, as I saw him frequently during his last months, practically once or twice every week.[5]

Ferenczi's stepdaughter, Mrs. Elma Lauvrik, who also was with Ferenczi until his death, wrote me a statement entirely confirming Dr. Thompson's and Dr. Balint's descriptions.

I have given such a detailed description of the fantastic constructions of Dr. Jones, partly in order to defend the memory of gifted and devoted men who can no longer defend themselves, and partly to show in a concrete example the party-line spirit to be found in certain quarters of the psychoanalytic movement. If one previously suspected the psychoanalytic

[5] Personal communication.

movement of such a spirit, then Jones's work, especially his treatment of Rank and Ferenczi in the third volume, confirms this suspicion in all details.

The question that arises now is: *How could psychoanalysis, a theory and a therapy, be transformed into this kind of fanatical movement?* The answer is to be found only by an examination of Freud's motives in developing the psychoanalytic movement.

Indeed, superficially seen, Freud was only the creator of a new *therapy for mental illness*, and this was the subject matter to which his main interest and all his efforts were devoted. However, if we look more closely, we find that behind this concept of a medical therapy for the cure of neurosis was an entirely different intention, rarely expressed by Freud and probably rarely even conscious. This hidden, implicit concept dealt primarily not with the cure of mental illness, but with something that transcended the concept of cure and illness. What was this something?

It was certainly not medicine. Freud wrote:

> After forty-one years of medical activity my self-knowledge tells me that I have never been a doctor in the proper sense. I became a doctor through being compelled to deviate from my original purpose; and the triumph of my life lies in my having, after a long, roundabout journey, found my way to my earliest path.

What was this earliest path to which Freud found his way back? He says it very clearly in the same paragraph: "In my youth I felt an overpowering need to *understand something of the riddles of the world in which we live, and perhaps even to contribute something to their solution.*" [italics added]

Interest in the riddles of the world and the wish to contribute something to their solution were quite active in Freud while he was in high school, especially during the last years, and he himself reports: "In the powerful influence of a school friendship with a boy rather my senior, who grew up to be a well-known politician, I developed a wish to study law like him, and to engage in social activities." This school friend, a Socialist, Heinrich Braun, was to become a leader in the Socialist movement. As Freud reports elsewhere, this was the time when the first bourgeois ministers were appointed by the Emperor, which aroused great jubilation in the homes of the liberal middle class, especially among the Jewish intelligentsia. By that time Freud had become greatly interested in the problems of socialism, in a future as a political leader, and he intended to study law as a first step in this direction. Even in the years when Freud worked as an assistant in a physiological laboratory he was fully aware that he must devote himself to a cause. In 1881 he wrote his fiancée:

> Philosophy, which I have always pictured as my goal and refuge in my old age, gains every day in attraction, as do human affairs all together, or any cause to which I could give my devotion at all costs; but the fear of the supreme uncertainty of all political and local matters keeps me from that sphere.

However, Freud's political interest—if we use the word "interest" in a rather broad sense—his identification with leaders who were either conquerors or the great benefactors of the human race, was by no means of so recent a date as his last years in high school. Already as a boy he had had a great admiration for Hannibal, which led to an identification with him that continued into his later life, as is clearly recognizable from his own reports. Freud's identification with Moses was perhaps even more profound and lasted longer. There is proof for this assertion. Suffice it to say here that Freud identified himself with Moses, who led a mass of ignorant people into a better life, a life of reason and the control of passion. Another indication of the same attitude was Freud's interest in 1910 in joining an "International Fraternity for Ethics and Culture". Jones reports that

Freud asked Jung whether he thought such a move feasible, and that only after Jung's negative response did he drop the idea. However, the International Psychoanalytic Movement, which was founded shortly thereafter, was to become a direct continuation of the idea of an International Fraternity for Ethics and Culture.

What were the aims and what was the dogma of this movement? Freud has expressed it perhaps most clearly in the sentence: "Where there was Id—there shall be Ego." His aim was the control of irrational passions by reason: the liberation of man from passion, within human possibilities. He studied the sources of the passions in order to help man to dominate them. His aim was truth, the knowledge of reality; to him this knowledge was man's only guiding light on earth. These aims were the traditional aims of rationalism, of the Enlightenment, and of puritan ethics. It was the genius of Freud that he connected them with a new psychological insight into the dimension of the hidden and irrational sources of human action.

In many of Freud's formulations it becomes visible that Freud's interest transcended that of a medical cure in itself. He speaks of psychoanalytic therapy as of "the liberation of the human being", of the analyst as one who must serve as a "model" and act as a "teacher"; and he states that "the relationship between analyst and patient is based on love of truth, that is, an acknowledgment of reality, that it precludes any kind of sham or deception".

What follows from all this? While consciously Freud was only a scientist and a therapist, unconsciously he was—and wanted to be—one of the great cultural-ethical leaders of the twentieth century. He wanted to conquer the world with his rationalistic-puritan dogma and to lead man to the only—and very limited—salvation he was capable of: the conquest of passion by intellect. To Freud, this, not any religion or any political solution like socialism, was the *only* valid answer to the problem of man.

Freud's movement was imbued with the enthusiasm of

eighteenth and nineteenth century rationalism and liberalism. It was Freud's tragic fate that this movement became popular after World War I among the urban middle class and the intelligentsia who were lacking in faith and in political or philosophical radicalism. Thus psychoanalysis became the substitute for radical philosophical and political interest, a new creed which demanded little from its adherents except learning the nomenclature.

It is exactly this function which has made psychoanalysis so popular today. The bureaucracy which inherited Freud's mantle capitalizes on this popularity, but it inherited little of his greatness and of his real radicalism. Its members fought one another in petty intrigues and machinations, and the "official" myth about Ferenczi and Rank serves to eliminate the only two productive and imaginative disciples among the original group who had remained after Adler's and Jung's defections. But I believe that, if psychoanalysis is to follow and develop the basic discoveries of Freud, it must revise from the standpoint of humanistic and dialectic thinking many of his theories conceived in the spirit of nineteenth-century physiological materialism. Such a translation of Freud into a new key must be based on a dynamic view of man rooted in insights into the specific conditions of human existence. The humanistic aims of Freud, transcending illness and therapy, may then find a new and more adequate expression—but only if psychoanalysis ceases to be governed by a sterile bureaucracy and regains its original daring in the search for truth.

5

THE REVOLUTIONARY CHARACTER

The concept of the "revolutionary character" is a political-psychological one. In this respect it resembles the concept of the authoritarian character which was introduced into psychology about thirty years ago. The latter combined a political category, that of the authoritarian structure in state and family, with a psychological category, the character structure which forms the basis for such a political and social structure.

The concept of the authoritarian character was born out of certain political interests: around 1930 in Germany, we wanted to ascertain what the chances were for Hitler's being defeated by the majority of the population.[1] In 1930 the majority of the German population, especially the workers and employees, were

[1] The study was directed by myself and had a number of collaborators, including Dr. E. Schachtel. Dr. P. Lazarsfeld acted as statistical adviser for the Institute of Social Research at the University of Frankfurt, then directed by Dr. M. Horkheimer.

against Nazism. They were on the side of democracy, as had been demonstrated by political and shop-steward elections. The *question* was whether they would fight for their ideas in the event that it came to a fight. The *premise* was that it is one thing to have an opinion and another to have a conviction. Or, to put it differently, anyone can acquire an opinion, just as one can learn a foreign language or a foreign custom, but only those opinions which are rooted in the character structure of a person, behind which there is the energy contained in his character—only those opinions *become convictions*. The effect of ideas, while these are easy to accept if the majority proclaims them, depends to a large extent on the character structure of a person in a critical situation. Character, as Heraclitus said and Freud demonstrated, is that fate of man. The character structure decides what kind of an idea a man will choose and also decides the force of the idea he has chosen. This is, indeed, the great importance in Freud's concept of character—that it transcends the traditional concept of behaviour and speaks of that behaviour which is dynamically charged, so that a man not only thinks in certain ways, but his very thought is rooted in his inclinations and emotions.

The question which we asked at that time was: To what extent do German workers and employees have a character structure which is opposite to the authoritarian idea of Nazism? And that implied still another question: to what extent will the German workers and employees, in the critical hour, fight Nazism? A study was made, and the result was that, roughly speaking, 10 per cent of the German workers and employees had what we call an authoritarian character structure; about 15 per cent had a democratic character structure, and the vast majority—about 75 percent—were people whose character structure was a mixture of both extremes.[2] The theoretical assumption was that the

[2] The method used was to examine the individually formulated answers to an open-ended questionnaire, by interpreting their unintended, unconscious

authoritarians would be ardent Nazis, the "democratic" ones militant anti-Nazis, and that the majority would be neither one nor the other. These theoretical assumptions turned out to be more or less accurate, as events in the years between 1933 and 1945 showed.[3]

For our purpose now it may suffice to say that the authoritarian character structure is the character structure of a person whose sense of strength and identity is based on a symbiotic subordination to authorities, and at the same time a symbiotic domination of those submitted to his authority. That is to say, the authoritarian character feels himself strong when he can submit and be part of an authority which (to some extent backed by reality), is inflated, is deified, and when at the same time he can inflate himself by incorporating those subject to his authority. This is a state of sado-masochistic symbiosis which gives him a sense of strength and a sense of identity. By being part of the "big" (whatever it is), he becomes big; if he were alone, by himself, he would shrink to nothing. For this very reason a threat to authority and a threat to his authoritarian structure is for the authoritarian character a threat to himself—a threat to his sanity. Hence he is forced to fight against this threat to authoritarianism as he would fight against a threat to his life or to his sanity.

In referring now to the concept of the *revolutionary character*, I should like to begin by saying what I believe the revolutionary

meaning, in distinction to the manifest answer. If a man, for instance, answered the question "Which men in history he admired most?" by saying "Alexander the Great, Caesar, Napoleon, Marx, and Lenin," we interpreted the answer as "authoritarian", because the combination shows that he admired dictators and military leaders. If the answer was "Socrates, Pasteur, Kant, Marx, and Lenin", we classified him as democratic because he admired benefactors of mankind and not people with power.

[3] The whole subject was treated later, with more refinement of method than in the original study, in an outstanding work by T. W. Adorno and others, *The Authoritarian Character*, Harper Bros., 1950.

character is *not*. Quite obviously the revolutionary character is not a person who participates in revolutions. This is exactly the point of difference between behaviour and character in the Freudian dynamic sense. Anyone can, for a number of reasons, participate in a revolution regardless of what he feels, provided he acts for the revolution. But the fact that he *acts* as a revolutionary tells us little about his character.

The second point of what a revolutionary character is *not*, is slightly more complicated. The revolutionary character is not a *rebel*. What do I mean by this?[4] I would define the rebel as the person who is deeply resentful of authority for not being appreciated, for not being loved, for not being accepted. A rebel is one who wants to overthrow authority out of his resentment and, as a result, to make himself the authority in place of the one he has overthrown. And very often, at the very moment when he reaches his aim, he will make friends with the very authority he was fighting so bitterly before.

The characterological type of the rebel is quite well known in the political history of the twentieth century. I take a figure like Ramsay MacDonald, for instance, who started out as a pacifist and a conscientious objector. When he had acquired sufficient power, he betrayed the Labour Party and joined the very authorities he had been fighting for so many years, saying to his friend and former comrade, Snowden, on the very day of his entering the National Government, "On this day, every Duchess in London will want to kiss me on both cheeks". Here you have the classic type of rebel who uses rebellion in order to become an authority.

Sometimes it takes years to accomplish this; sometimes things go faster. For example, if you take a personality like the unfortunate Laval in France, who started out as a rebel, you may

[4] I have been able to deal with this in greater detail in my earlier work, *The Fear of Freedom*, Routledge & Kegan Paul, 1942.

recall that only a very short time elapsed until he had acquired enough political capital to be ready to sell out. There are many others whom I could name, but the psychological mechanism is always the same. You might say that twentieth-century political life is a cemetery containing the moral graves of people who started out as alleged revolutionaries and who turned out to be nothing but opportunistic rebels.

There is something else that the revolutionary character is not, and which is somewhat more complicated than the concept of the rebel: he is not a *fanatic*. Revolutionaries, in the behavioural sense, are often fanatics, and at this point the difference between political behaviour and character structure is particularly apparent—at least as I see the character of the revolutionary. What do I mean by fanatic? I do not mean a man who has a conviction. (I might mention that today it has become fashionable to call anyone who has a conviction a "fanatic", and anyone who has no conviction, or whose convictions are easily expendable, a "realist".)

I think one can describe the fanatic clinically as a person who is exceedingly narcissistic—in fact, a person who is close to psychosis (depression or melancholia, often blended with paranoid trends); a person who is completely unrelated, as any pschotic person is, to the world outside. But the fanatic has found a solution which saves him from manifest psychosis. He has chosen a cause, whatever it may be—political, religious or any other—and he has deified this cause. He has made this cause an idol. In this manner, by complete submission to his idol, he receives a passionate sense of life, a meaning of life; for in his submission he identifies himself with the idol, which he has inflated and made into an absolute.

If we want to choose a symbol for the fanatic, it would be *burning ice*. He is a person who is passionate and extremely cold at the same time. He is utterly unrelated to the world, and yet filled with burning passion, the passion of participation in and submission to the Absolute. In order to recognize the character of a fanatic one must listen not so much to what he says, but watch for that particular glitter in his eye, that cold passion, which is the paradox of the fanatic: namely an utter lack of relatedness blended with passionate worship of his idol. The fanatic is close to what the Prophets called an "idol worshipper". Needless to say, the fanatic has always played a great role in history; and very often he has posed as a revolutionary, because very often what he says is precisely—or sounds precisely—like what a revolutionary might say.

I have tried to explain what I consider the revolutionary character *not* to be. I think that the characterological concept of the revolutionary is an important concept today—just as important, perhaps, as the concept of the authoritarian character. Indeed, we live in an era of revolutions which began about two hundred and fifty years ago, commencing with the political rebellions starting with the English Revolution, the French and the American, and on to the social revolutions in Russia, in China and—continuing to the present time—Latin America.

In this revolutionary era the word "revolutionary" has remained very attractive in many places in the world, as a positive qualification for many political movements. In fact, all these movements which use the word "revolutionary" *claim* very similar aims: namely, that they fight for freedom and independence. But in reality some do and some do not; by which I mean that while some do in reality fight for freedom and independence, in others the revolutionary slogan is used in order to fight for the establishment of authoritarian regimes, but with a different elite in the saddle.

How could we define a revolution? We could define it in the dictionary sense by simply saying that a revolution is the overthrow, peaceful or violent, of an existing government and its replacement by a new government. This, of course, is a very formal political definition and not particularly meaningful. We might, in a somewhat more Marxist sense, define a revolution as the replacement of an existing order by an historically more progressive one. Of course, the question always arises here as to who decides what is "historically more progressive". Usually it is the winner, at least in his own country.

Finally, we might define revolution in a psychological sense, saying that a revolution is a political movement led by people with revolutionary characters, and attracting people with revolutionary characters. That, of course, is not much of a definition, but it is a useful statement from the standpoint of this paper, since it puts all the emphasis on the question now to be discussed: namely, what is a revolutionary character?

The most fundamental characteristic of the "revolutionary character" is that he is *independent*—that he is *free*. It is easy to see that independence is the opposite of symbiotic attachment to the powerful ones above, and to the powerless ones below, as I previously described in speaking about the authoritarian character. But this does not clarify sufficiently what is meant by "independent" and "freedom". The difficulty lies precisely in the fact that the words "freedom" and "independence" are used today with the implication that in a democratic system everybody is free and independent. This concept of independence and freedom has its roots in the middle-class revolution against the feudal order, and it has gained new strength by being contrasted with totalitarian regimes. During the feudal and monarchical absolutist order, the individual was neither free nor independent. He was subject to either traditional or arbitrary rules and commands from those above him. The victorious bourgeois revolutions in Europe and America brought political freedom and independence for the individual. This freedom was a "freedom *from*"—an independence *from* political authorities.

No doubt this was an important development, even though today's industrialism has created new forms of dependence in the sprawling bureaucracies which are in contrast to the unfettered initiative and independence of the businessman in the nineteenth century. However, the problem of independence and freedom goes much deeper than freedom and independence in the above-mentioned sense. Actually the problem of independence is the most fundamental aspect of human development, provided we see it in its full depth and scope.

The new-born infant is still one with his environment. For him, the world outside does not yet exist as a reality separate from himself. But even when the child can recognize objects outside of himself, he still remains helpless for a long time, and could not survive without the help of mother and father. This prolonged helplessness of the human, in contrast to the animal young, is one basis for his development, but it also teaches the child to lean on power—and to fear power.

Normally in the years from birth to puberty the parents are the ones who represent power and its twofold aspect: to help and to punish. Around the time of puberty the young person has reached a stage of development in which he can fend for himself (certainly in the simpler agrarian societies), and does not necessarily owe his social existence any longer to his parents. He can become economically independent from them. In many primitive societies independence (particularly from mother) is expressed by initiation rites which, however, do not touch the dependence on the clan in its male aspect. The maturing of sexuality is another factor in furthering the process of emancipation from the parents. Sexual desire and sexual satisfaction bind a person to those outside his family. The sexual act itself is one which neither father nor mother can help, in which the young person is all on his own.

Even in societies where the satisfaction of the sexual desire is postponed until five or ten years after puberty, the awakened sexual desire creates longings for independence, and produces conflicts with parental and social authorities. The normal person acquires this degree of independence in the years after puberty. But it is an undeniable fact that this kind of independence, even though a person may earn his own living, marry, and bring up children of his own, does not mean that he has become truly free and independent. He is still, as an adult, rather helpless and in many ways trying to find powers to protect him and give him certainty. The price he pays for this help is that he makes himself dependent on them, loses his freedom and slows down the process of his growth. He borrows his thought from them, his feelings, his goals, his values—although he lives under the illusion that it is he who thinks, feels, and makes his choices.

Full freedom and independence exist only when the individual thinks, feels, and decides for himself. He can do so authentically only when he has reached a productive relatedness to the world outside himself, which permits him to respond authentically. This concept of freedom and independence is to be found in the thought of the radical mystics, as well as in that of Marx. The most radical of the Christian mystics, Meister Eckhart, says: "What is my life? That which is moved from within by itself. That which is moved from without does not live."[5] Or, ". . . if a man derives or receives anything from outside, it is wrong. One should not apprehend God nor consider Him outside oneself, but as our own and as what is in ourselves."[6]

Marx, in a similar, though non-theological vein, says:

> A being does not regard himself as independent unless he is his own master, and he is only his own master when he owes his existence to himself. A man who lives by the favour of another considers himself a dependent being. But I live

[5] Sermon XVII, *Meister Eckhart, An Introduction to the Study of his Works, with an Anthology of his Sermons*, selected by James M. Clark, Thomas Nelson & Sons, London, 1957, p. 235.

[6] Ibid., p. 189. A very similar attitude is to be found in Zen Buddhism on the question of independence from God, Buddha, or any other authorities.

> completely by another person's favour when I owe to him not only the continuance of my life but also *its creation*; when he is its *source*. My life has necessarily such a cause outside itself, if it is not my own creation.[7]

Or, as Marx said somewhere else:

> Man is independent only if he affirms his individuality as a total man in each of his relations to the world, seeing, hearing, smelling, tasting, feeling, thinking, willing, loving—in short, if he affirms and expresses all organs of his individuality.

Independence and freedom are the realization of individuality, not only emancipation from coercion nor freedom in commercial matters.

The problem of each individual is precisely that of the level of freedom he has reached. The fully awakened, productive man is a free man because he can live authentically—his own self being the source of his life. (It should not be necessary to say that this does not mean that the independent man is an isolated man, for the growth of personality occurs in the process of being related to and interested in others and the world. But this relatedness is entirely different from dependence.) While for Marx the problem of independence as self-realization leads to his criticism of bourgeois society, Freud dealt with the same problem within the framework of his theory, in terms of the Oedipus complex.

Freud, believing that the way to mental health lies in the overcoming of the incestuous fixation to mother, stated that mental health and maturity are based on emancipation and independence. But for him this process was initiated by the fear

[7] K. Marx, *Economic and Philosophical Manuscripts*, transl. by T. B. Bottomore, in E. Fromm, *Marx's Concept of Man*, Frederick Ungar Publishing Co., New York, 1961, p. 138.

of castration by father, and ended by incorporating father's commands and prohibitions into one's self (Superego). Hence the independence remained partial from one's mother; dependence on one's father and on social authorities continued through the Superego.

The revolutionary character is the one who is identified with humanity and therefore transcends the narrow limits of his own society, and who is able, because of this, to criticize his or any other society from the standpoint of reason and humanity. He is not caught in the parochial worship of that culture which he happens to be born in, which is nothing but an accident of time and geography. He is able to look at his environment with the open eyes of a man who is awake and who finds his criteria of judging the accidental in that which is not accidental (reason), in the norms which exist in and for the human race.

The revolutionary character is identified with humanity. He has also a deep "reverence for life", to use Albert Schweitzer's term, a deep affinity with and love for life. It is true, as far as we are like all other animals, that we cling to life and fight death. But *clinging* to life is something quite different from *loving* life. This may even be more apparent if we consider the fact that there is a type of personality which is attracted by death, destruction and decay, rather than by life. (Hitler is a good historical example of this). This type of character can be called necrophilous, to use Unamuno's expression in his famous answer in 1936 to a Franco general, whose favourite motto was "Long live death".

The attraction to death and destruction may not be conscious in a person, yet its presence can be inferred from his actions. To strangle, squelch, and destroy life gives, to him, the same satisfaction as the life-loving person finds in making life grow, expand, and develop. Necrophilia is the *true* perversion, that of aiming at destruction while one is alive.

The revolutionary character thinks and feels in what might be called a "critical mood"—in a critical key, to use a symbol from music. The Latin motto *De omnibus est dubitandum* (one has to doubt everything) is a very important part of his response to the world. This critical mood I am discussing is by no means anything like cynicism, but it is an insight into reality, in contrast to the fictions which are made a substitute for reality.[8]

The non-revolutionary character will be particularly prone to believe something which is announced by the majority. The person in the critical mood will react precisely in the opposite way. He will be particularly critical when he hears the judgment of the majority which is that of the market place, of those who have power. Of course, if more people were true Christians as they claim to be, they would have no difficulty in maintaining such an attitude, because, indeed, this critical approach to accepted standards was that of Jesus. This critical mood was also the mood of Socrates. It was the mood of the prophets, and of many of the men whom we worship in one way or another. Only when they have been dead for a long enough time—safely and sufficiently dead, that is—is it safe to praise them.

The "critical mood" is one in which a person is sensitive to the cliché or so-called "common sense", that common sense which repeats the same nonsense over and over, and makes sense only because everybody repeats it. Perhaps the critical mood I am talking about is not something which you can easily define, but if one experiments with oneself and others, one very easily discovers the person who has such a critical mood and the person who has not.

How many millions of people, for instance, really believe that by the atomic arms race peace can be served? It is against all our experience of the past. How many people believe that if the siren sounds—although shelters have been built in the great metropolitan cities of the United States—they could save

[8] Cf. the more detailed discussion of this point in E. Fromm, *Beyond the Chains of Illusion*, Simon and Schuster, New York, 1963.

themselves? They know that they would have no more than fifteen minutes of time. One does not need to be an alarmist to foresee that he would be trampled to death trying to reach the doors of the shelter in those fifteen minutes. Still, apparently, millions of people are able to believe that our famous underground shelters are capable of saving them from 50 or 100-megaton bombs. Why? Because they are not in a critical mood. A little boy of five (children that age usually have more of a critical attitude than adults) if told the same story, would probably question it. Most adults are sufficiently "educated" not to be in critical mood, and hence believe to be "sense" things which are plain nonsense.

In addition to having a critical mood, the revolutionary character has a particular relationship to power. He is not a dreamer who does not know that power can kill you, compel you, and even pervert you. But he has a particular relationship to power in another sense. For him power never becomes sanctified, it never takes on the role of truth, or of the moral and good. This is perhaps one of the most, if not the most important problem of today: namely, the relationship of persons to power. It is not a question of knowing what power is. Nor is the problem the lack of realism—of underestimating the role and functions of power. It is a question of whether power is sanctified or not, and of whether a person is morally impressed by power. He who is morally impressed by power is never in a critical mood, and he is never a revolutionary character.

The revolutionary character is capable of saying "No". Or, to put it differently, the revolutionary character is a person capable of disobedience. He is someone for whom disobedience can be a virtue. To explain this, I might begin with a statement that sounds rather sweeping: human history began with an act of disobedience and might end with an act of obedience. What do I mean by this? In saying that human history began with an act of disobedience, I refer to Hebrew and Greek mythology. In the story of Adam and Eve, there is a command by God not to eat of the fruit, and man—or rather, to be quite fair, woman—is able to say "No". She is capable of disobeying and even of persuading the man to share her disobedience. What is the result? In the myth man is driven out of Paradise—that is to say, man is driven out of the pre-individualistic, pre-conscious, pre-historical and, if you wish, pre-human situation, a situation which could be compared to that of the foetus in the mother's womb. And he is driven out on the road to history.

In the language of the myth he is not *permitted* to return. He is, in fact, *unable* to return. Because once his awareness of himself has been awakened, once he is aware of himself as being separate from man, from nature, man cannot return again to the primordial harmony which existed before his awareness ever began. With this first act of disobedience, man's history begins, and this first act of disobedience is the first act of freedom.

The Greeks used a different symbol, the symbol of Prometheus. It is Prometheus who steals the fire from the gods and commits a crime, who commits an act of disobedience, and with the act of bringing fire to man, human history—or human civilization—begins.

Both the Hebrews and the Greeks taught that human endeavour and human history began with an act of disobedience.

And why do I say that human history may end by an act of obedience? Here I am unfortunately not speaking mythologically, but very realistically. If an atomic war should destroy in two or three years' time half the human population, and lead to a period of complete barbarization—or if this should happen ten years from now and possibly destroy all life on this earth—this will be due to an act of obedience. That is, the obedience of the men who push the button to the men who give the orders, and the obedience to ideas which make it possible to think in terms of such madness.

Disobedience is a dialectical concept, because actually every act of disobedience is an act of obedience, and every act of obedience is an act of disobedience. What do I mean by this? Every act of disobedience, unless it is empty rebelliousness, is obedience to another principle. I am disobedient to the idol because I am obedient to God. I am disobedient to Caesar because I am obedient to God, or, if you speak in non-theological language, because I am obedient to principles and values, to my conscience, I may be disobedient to the State because I am obedient to the laws of humanity. And if I am obedient, then indeed I am always disobedient to something else. The question is not really one of disobedience or obedience, but one of disobedience or obedience to what and to whom.

It follows from what I have said that the revolutionary character, in the sense in which I am using this word, is not necessarily a character type which has its place only in politics. The revolutionary character exists, indeed, in politics, but also in religion, in art and in philosophy. Buddha, the Prophets, Jesus, Giordano Bruno, Meister Eckhart, Galileo, Marx and Engels, Einstein, Schweitzer, Russell—they are all revolutionary characters. In fact, you find the revolutionary character also in a man who is in none of these fields; in a man whose "yes" is "yes", and whose "no" is "no". He is the one who is capable of seeing reality, as the little boy did in Andersen's fairy tale of the Emperor's clothes: he saw that the Emperor was naked, and what he said was faithful to what he had seen.

The nineteenth century, perhaps, was a period in which it was easier to recognize disobedience. Because the nineteenth century was a time of overt authority in family life and in the State; hence there was a place for the revolutionary character. The twentieth century is a very different period. It is a century of the modern industrial system that creates the organization man, a system of vast bureaucracies which insist on the smooth functioning of those submitted to them, but by manipulation rather than by force. The managers of these bureaucracies claim that this submission to their orders is a voluntary one and try to persuade all of us, especially by the amount of material satisfaction that they offer, that we like to do what we are supposed to do. The organization man is not one who disobeys; he does not even know that he is obeying. How can he think of disobeying when he is not even conscious of being obedient? He is just one of the "boys", one of the crowd. He is "sound". He thinks and does what is "reasonable"—even if it kills him and his children, and his grandchildren. Hence it is much more difficult for a man of the contemporary bureaucratic industrial age to be disobedient, or to develop the revolutionary character, than it was for the man of the nineteenth century.

We live in an age in which the logic of the balance sheet, the logic of the production of things, has been extended to the life of human beings. Human beings have become numbers, just as things have become numbers. Things and men have become quantities in the process of production.

To repeat: It is very difficult to be disobedient if one is not even aware of being obedient. To put it differently, who can disobey an electronic computer? How can we say "No" to the kind of philosophy whose ideal is to act like an electronic computer, without will, without feeling, without passion?

Obedience today is not recognized as obedience, because it is rationalized as "common sense", as a matter of accepting objective necessities. If it is necessary to build up, both in the East and in the West, a fantastically destructive armament, who could disobey? Who would feel like saying "No", if it was all presented not as an act of human will, but as an act of objective necessity?

There is another relevant aspect of our current situation. In this industrial system which, I believe, is growing more and more similar in the West and in the Soviet bloc, the individual is frightened to death by the power of the big bureaucracies, by the bigness of everything, the State, the industrial bureaucracy, and the trade union bureaucracy. He is not only frightened, he feels himself utterly small. Who is the David who can say "No" to Goliath? Who is the little man who can say "No" to that which has become magnified in bigness and power a thousandfold, as compared to that which used to be authority only fifty or a hundred years ago? The individual is intimidated and glad to accept authority. He accepts the orders he is given in the name of common sense and reason, in order not to feel that he has submitted—in order to eliminate the possible thought that his submission might cost his own life and the life of mankind.

To sum up: by "revolutionary character" I refer not to a behavioural concept, but to a dynamic concept. One is not a "revolutionary" in this characterological sense because he utters revolutionary phrases, nor because he participates in a revolution. The revolutionary, in this sense, is the man who has emancipated himself from the ties of blood and soil, from his mother and his father, from special loyalties to State, class, race, party or religion. The revolutionary character is a humanist in the sense that he experiences in himself all of humanity, and that nothing human is alien to him. He loves and respects life. He is a sceptic *and* a man of faith.

He is a sceptic because he suspects ideologies as covering up undesirable realities. He is a man of faith because he believes in that which potentially exists, although it has not yet been born. He can say "No" and be disobedient, precisely because he can say "Yes" and obey those principles which are genuinely his own. He is not half asleep, but fully awake to the personal and social realities around him. He is independent, what he is he owes to his own effort; he is free and not a servant to anyone.

This summary may suggest that what I have been describing is the mental health and well-being, rather than the concept of a revolutionary character. Indeed, the description given is that of the sane, alive, mentally healthy person. My assertion is that the sane person in an insane world, the fully developed human being in a crippled world, the fully awake person in a half asleep world—is precisely the revolutionary character. Once all are awake, there need no longer be any prophets or revolutionary characters—there will be only fully developed human beings.

The majority of people, of course, have never been revolutionary characters. But the reason why we are no longer living in caves is precisely because there have always been enough revolutionary characters in human history to get us out of the caves and their equivalents. There are, however, many others who pretend to be revolutionaries when, in fact, they are rebels, authoritarians or political opportunists. I believe psychologists have an important function in studying the characterological differences behind these various types of political ideologists. But in order to do so properly they must, I fear, have some of the qualities this essay has been trying to describe: they must themselves be revolutionary characters.

6

MEDICINE AND THE ETHICAL PROBLEM OF MODERN MAN

What do we mean by ethics?

The word "ethics" comes from a root which means, originally, custom, and eventually ethics comes to mean the science dealing with the ideals of human relatedness. This confusion between custom and ideals still exists in the minds of many people.

Most people today consciously think of ethics in terms of an ideal, of ethical norms, when they really mean that that which is the custom is also that which is good; while we consciously mean by ethical norm an "ought", unconsciously we really think that the right is that which is accepted. And, as we know, the accepted is also the most comfortable solution, except from the standpoint of one's conscience.

Sometimes ethics refers only to behaviour; then what is meant by it is a code—a code of certain desirable behaviour. Then, of course, you can divide ethics. You can speak of medical ethics, of business ethics, or military ethics. In all these instances you are really speaking of a code of behaviour relating to, or valid for, a certain situation. Of course, this is perfectly all right; I prefer people who have a code to those who do not, and I prefer good codes to bad codes. But if we mean by ethics what was meant by the term in the great philosophical or religious tradition, then ethics is not a code of behaviour valid for certain fields. In this tradition, ethics refers to a particular orientation which is rooted in man and which, therefore, is not valid in reference to this or that person or to this or that situation but to all human beings. Indeed, if the Buddhists are right, it is valid not only with regard to human beings but for everything that is. Conscience is the organ of this ethical attitude; if we speak of ethics in the sense of the great philosophical and religious tradition of the East and West, then ethics is not a code; it is a matter of conscience.

If we accept this viewpoint, then there is no such thing as medical ethics. There is only *universal human ethics applied to specific human situations*. If, on the other hand, we separate medical ethics from the universal problem of ethics, then there is danger that medical ethics might degenerate into a code which serves essentially the function of protecting the interests of the medical guild against the patient.

At this point it is appropriate to say something more about conscience. It is important to keep in mind a distinction between authoritarian conscience and humanistic conscience.[1] By authoritarian conscience I mean, more or less, what Freud meant by superego, a term much more popular today than the term "conscience". Authoritarian conscience, or superego, is the internalized power of the father, originally; later it is the internalized authority of society. Instead of being afraid of father punishing me, I have internalized father's commands so that I do not have to wait for the terrible experience; I hear father's voice

[1] I have analyzed these two types of conscience in greater detail in *Man For Himself*, Routledge & Kegan Paul, 1949, pp. 143–172.

within me and I do not risk any unpleasant event. I am warned before-hand because father is in me. This concept of the internalized authority of father and of society is valid for what many people call their conscience. Freud's explanation of the psychological mechanism, I think, is most ingenious and very true. The question arises, however: is that all, or is there another conscience that is quite different?

Now, the second type of conscience, which is not internalized authority, I called humanistic conscience, referring to the philosophic or religious humanistic tradition. This conscience is an inner voice that calls us back to ourselves. By this "ourselves" is meant the human core common to all men, that is, certain basic characteristics of man which cannot be violated or negated without serious consequences.

Many scientists today feel that this is nonsense, that there is no such thing as "the nature of man". They think it all depends on where you live. If you are a headhunter, you like to kill people and to shrink their heads; and if you are living in Hollywood, you like to make money and to see yourself in the newspapers; and so on. They believe that there is nothing in human nature which says you should do one thing and not do another. Psychoanalysts and psychiatrists should be able to report differently; they could state that there are, indeed, certain basic elements which are part of human nature and which will react in the very same way as our body reacts if its laws are violated. If a pathological process occurs in our body, usually we have pain; and if a pathological process occurs in our souls—that is to say, if something happens in our souls which violates something deeply ingrained in human nature—then something else happens: we have a guilty conscience. Now, if people can't sleep, they take pills. If they have pain, they can take some other pills. The guilty conscience is tranquillized in the many ways our culture offers for such purpose. Nevertheless, the guilty conscience, though it may be unconscious, has many ways of expressing itself, and has a language which sometimes is just as painful as physically conditioned pain.

Doctors and medical students, since they have to deal so much with physical pain and physical symptoms, should be especially attentive to what has been learned in regard to mental pain and mental symptoms. For instance, a person who in his life negates completely what Albert Schweitzer has called "reverence for life", who is utterly cruel, utterly inhuman, utterly without kindness, utterly without love, is brought to the verge of insanity. When he goes on and on, he is afraid of becoming insane, and sometimes he does become insane. Sometimes he develops a neurosis which saves him from insanity; even some of the worst men on this earth need to keep the illusion—and maybe not even entirely the illusion—that there is something human and something kind in them, because if they could not feel that any more, then they would not feel human any more and they would feel, indeed, close to insanity.

We can easily find some striking examples of this. Dr. Gustave Gilbert, a psychologist who interviewed Goering and other captured Nazi leaders for a year until the last day of their lives, has told of his experiences. He tells how a man like Goering would beg him to come every day and would say, "Look, I'm not so bad as all this. I am not as bad as Hitler; Hitler killed women and children. I didn't. Please believe me." He knew that he was to die. The man to whom he talked was a young American psychologist whose opinion about him was of no consequence whatsoever. He was not speaking to an audience, yet he could not stand the idea of facing himself, once his power had vanished, as an utterly inhuman being. A similar story is provided by an American press representative who lived for some time in Moscow. It concerns a man named Jagoda, who was Chief of the Secret Police before he was killed by those who were themselves to be killed later. Jagoda was certainly responsible for the death and torture of hundreds of thousands of people. According to the reporter, he had near Moscow an orphanage which was one of the most beautiful places anywhere in the world—orphans were treated with freedom, with love, with every consideration. One day Jagoda said to this press representative: "Will you do me a great favour and write an article about my orphanage here, and please write it for a certain magazine in New York." The reporter looked at him in surprise, and the Chief of the Secret Police explained: "You see, I have an uncle in Brooklyn, my mother's brother, who reads that magazine. My mother thinks that I am the devil. If my uncle reads your article, he will write my mother and I will feel better." The reporter wrote the article. He states that as a result, Jagoda spared a number of lives and remained grateful to the reporter to the end of his life.

The problem was not Jagoda's mother; it was his conscience. He couldn't stand the complete inhumaneness of his life.

A Viennese psychiatrist who visited East Germany reports that psychiatrists there speak of a neurotic breakdown which they call "functionaries' disease". They refer to the disease which takes the form of neurotic breakdown in Communist functionaries who have been in the "service" for a long time. At a certain point there is something they cannot stand. We could collect a great deal of material in all countries and all cultures that illustrates the same principle, namely, that you cannot live inhumanly all your life without suffering severe reactions; just as you cannot constantly undernourish your body and not die eventually, though not immediately.

I have given examples from Stalinist Russia and Nazi Germany; but I do not mean to imply that we do not have similar problems in the United States. Here, and throughout the Western world, our problem is not cruelty, it is not destructiveness: it is *boredom*. Life is meaningless. People live, but feel they are not alive; life runs out like sand. And a person who is alive and, consciously or unconsciously, knows that he is not alive, feels repercussions which, if he has retained a little sensitivity and aliveness, often result in a neurosis. And it is people like that who consult analysts today. At a conscious level, they are complaining about their unsatisfactory marriage or their poor job or something else; but if you ask what is behind the complaints, the answer is usually that life does not make sense. Such people sense that they live in a world in which they should be excited, interested, active, yet they seem to be dead and inhuman.

If I am really to deal with the ethical problem of our time—the problem of modern man, I must begin by saying that, although the ethical norms for human conduct are the same for all men, nevertheless each age and each culture has its particular problems and therefore its particular ethical aims. I will not attempt to discuss the problems of the ethical aims of various ages; I will discuss the ethical problems of the nineteenth century and those of the twentieth century.

The main ethical problems, the main sins of the nineteenth century, I believe, can be listed as follows: First, *exploitation*—one man was another man's food. Whether this exploitation referred to the worker, to the peasant, or to the Negro in the Congo or in the southern United States, one man used another man for food—not exactly cannibalistically, for he had better food—but he used another man's life energy to feed himself. The second moral problem of the nineteenth century was *authoritarianism*—men in power felt that by virtue of their power they had the right to command and to restrict other men. That was the authority of the father over his children, so beautifully described in Butler's *Way of All Flesh*; the authority of men over women; the authority of bosses over workers; and the authority of states over other states, especially over those whose inhabitants were of a different colour. The third problem was *inequality*. It was considered right that people on this globe and even within the same nation lived under material circumstances of utter inequality—that the sexes were not equal; that races were not equal, in spite of lip service to Christianity, which in its essence is a universal religion predicated on the concept that we all are the children of God.

Another vice of the nineteenth century, especially of the middle class, was *stinginess*, hoarding, saving of feelings and of things. Closely related to this hoarding attitude was an egotistic individualism: "My home is my castle"; "My property is me."

We tend to think of these vices as peculiar to the nineteenth century, and feel that we have indeed advanced far beyond our grandfathers. We no longer practise these vices, and we feel fine. Perhaps that is how every generation views its own ethical problems. Just as the French strategically fought World War II with the ideas of World War I, so every generation fights the moral issue in terms of the preceding generation. It sees very easily how wonderfully it has overcome certain vices, but it does not see that negation of what formerly existed is not in itself a fulfilment, and in a changing society and culture it does not recognize new vices because it is happy feeling that old vices have disappeared.

Let us go back over those nineteenth-century vices and discuss what has become of them. We have, indeed, no authority. Children can "express themselves" and do as they please. Workers are supposed to talk up and to express their feelings to paid psychologists, and no boss today would dare act at all like the way a boss fifty years ago acted. But we have no principles; we have no sense of values nor any standards of values.

I would like to introduce here a concept of the distinction between irrational and rational authority. By irrational authority I mean authority which is based on force, either physical or emotional, and the function of which is the exploitation of other persons, materially, emotionally, or otherwise. Rational authority is authority which is based on competence, and the function of which is to help another person accomplish a certain task. I think these authorities are greatly confused today. If little Johnny says to his mother, "Two and two are five", his mother may feel that she is inhibiting his freedom of expression if she insists that two and two are four. If she is very sophisticated, she may even rationalize that mathematical systems are not absolute, anyway, so "my Johnny is right after all".

When you recall Thoreau's paper, "Life Without Principles", written a hundred years ago, you may find it hard to believe that this is a problem of the twentieth century. Apparently it was already a problem in the nineteenth century. But if that was true in Thoreau's time, how much truer it is today! What Thoreau saw with great sensitivity was that people had opinions but no convictions, that they had facts but no principles. This development has continued, until today it has assumed frightening proportions and, I believe, also a frightening role for education. Progressive education was a reaction to the authoritarianism of the nineteenth century and, in defiance, was therefore a constructive achievement. But along with certain other trends in our culture it has deteriorated into a *laissez faire* in which no principle is recognized, no value is stated, and no hierarchy exists. I am thinking not of a hierarchy of power but a hierarchy of knowledge and respect for those who are better informed. Today we meet with the dogmatic assumption that spontaneity, originality, and individualism are necessarily in conflict with rational authority and a sense of accepted standards; one useful corrective might be familiarity with the Zen art of archery which tends to combine apparently contradictory attitudes.[2]

As to the second vice, hoarding, certainly we do not hoard. Hoarding would bring about a national catastrophe. Our economy is based on spending. And, of course, such moral changes very often are the result of certain economic changes. Our advertising industry is a constant appeal to spend, not to hoard. So

[2] Cf. Eugen Herrigel's fascinating book, *Zen in the Art of Archery*, Routledge & Kegan Paul, 1953, in which the author, a German philosopher, describes his experiences in studying this Zen art in Tokyo for seven years.

what do we do? We practise incessant consumption for consumption's sake. We all know this; it needs no discussion. A cartoon in *The New Yorker* makes my point: one man looks at the new cars with long fins and is annoyed; the man next to him says: "You may not be pleased, but if everybody weren't pleased, what would become of the American economy?" Actually our danger is not that of hoarding, but it is just as great—we are eternal consumers—receiving, receiving, receiving. Eight hours a day, whatever our position may be, we work; we are active. In our leisure time, however, we are completely lazy, with the passivity of consumers. The consumer attitude has now moved on from the field of economics to invade more and more the sphere of everyday life. We consume cigarettes and cocktails and books and television; we seem to be looking for the big nursing bottle which would provide total nourishment. Eventually we consume tranquillizers.

Inequality is the third vice which we seem to think we have overcome. Indeed the inequality which existed and was permitted in the nineteenth century is vanishing. Despite the vast amount that remains to be done, an objective observer will be impressed by the progress made toward the equality of races in America, especially in the years since World War II. Progress toward economic equality in the United States has also been considerable. But what have we arrived at? We have distorted the notion of equality into the notion of sameness. What did the concept of "equality" mean in the great humanistic tradition? It meant that we were equal in one sense: that *every man is an end in himself and must not be a means for the end of anyone else.* Equality is the condition in which no man must be a means, but every man is an end in himself, regardless of age, colour, sex. This was the humanistic definition of equality which was the basis, indeed, for the development of differences. Only if we are permitted to be different without being threatened with being treated as unequal, only then are we equal.

But what have we done? We have transformed the concept of equality into that of sameness. Actually we are afraid to be different because we are afraid that if we are different, we have no right to be here. I recently asked a man in his early thirties why he was so afraid of doing something worth while with his life, living intensely and with zest. After a moment's thought he said, "You know, I am really afraid because that would mean to be so different." Unfortunately, I believe that is true of many people.

Now this concept of equality, which has all the prestige, all the dignity, of a great philosophical and humanistic concept, is misused for one of the most degrading, inhuman, and dangerous aspects of our culture, namely, sameness, which means loss of individuality. You can see it perhaps in relationships between the sexes; you will find in the United States that the sexes have become "equal" to a point where the polarity between the sexes is equalized and the creative spark which springs only from the polarity of opposites gets lost. But unless that polarity is permitted to exist there can be no creativity, for it is in the meeting of the two poles that the spark of creativeness can appear.

In this transformation of nineteenth-century vices into twentieth-century vices—which are called virtues—we must also note the considerable elimination of egocentric individualism and exploitation. In no other country in the world has exploitation disappeared to the same extent as in the United States. Economists say that within a relatively short time results will be even more fantastic than they are now. Egocentric individualism hardly exists—nobody wants to be alone, everybody wants to be with somebody else, and people get panicky at the thought of being alone for even a little while. These vices have disappeared, but what has replaced them? Man experiences himself as a thing—as a commodity, himself and others. He experiences the life energy as capital to be invested for profit; and if it is profitable, he calls it success. We make machines which act like men and produce men who act like machines. The danger of the nineteenth century was that of becoming slaves; the danger of the twentieth century is not that we become slaves but that we become robots.

Originally all our material production was a means to an end. A means to the end of greater happiness—that is what we still claim. But actually, material production has become an end in itself, and we do not really know what to do with it. Take only one example: the wish to save time. When we have the time saved we are embarrassed because we do not know what to do with it, so we find ways and means to kill it; then we start saving it again. Man, in our culture, experiences himself not as an active subject, not as the centre of his world, not as a creator of his own acts but rather as a powerless *thing*. His own acts and their consequences have become his masters. Think of the symbol, if not of the gruesome reality, of the atomic bomb. Man worships the products of his own hands, the leaders of his own making, as if they were superior to him, rather than created by him. We believe we are Christians or Jews or whatever we may be, but actually we have fallen into a state of idolatry for which we find a better description in the Prophets than anywhere else. We do not offer sacrifice to Baal or Astarte, but we do worship things, production, success; we seem naïvely unaware that we are idolatrous, and think that we are sincere when we talk about God. Some people even try to combine religion and materialism until religion becomes a do-it-yourself method to greater success without the benefit of a psychiatrist. Indeed, things have become objects of "ultimate concern". And what is the result? The result is that man is empty, unhappy, bored.

When boredom is mentioned, people think that, of course, it is not nice to be bored, but they do not think it is a serious matter. I am convinced that boredom is one of the greatest tortures. If I were to imagine Hell, it would be the place where you were continually bored. In fact, people make a frantic effort to avoid boredom, running away to this, that, or the other, because their boredom is unbearable. If you have "your" neurosis and "your" analyst, it helps you feel less bored. Even if you have anxiety and compulsive symptoms, at least they are interesting! In fact, I am convinced that one of the motivations for having such things is escape from boredom.

I believe that the statement, "Man is not a thing", is the central topic of the ethical problem of modern man. Man is not a thing, and if you try to transform him into a thing, you damage him. Or, to quote Simone Weil: "Power is the capacity of transforming a man into a thing because you transform a living being into a corpse." A corpse is a thing. Man is not. Ultimate power—the power to destroy—is exactly the ultimate power of transforming life into a thing. Man cannot be taken apart and put together again; a thing can be. A thing is predictable; man is not. A thing cannot create. Man can. A thing has no self. Man has. Man has the capacity to say the most peculiar and difficult word in our language, the word "I". You know that children learn the word "I" relatively late; but after that we all say, without hesitation, "I think", "I feel", "I do". And if we examine what we really are saying—the reality of the statement—we find that it is not true. It would be much more correct to say, "It thinks in me", "It feels in me". If, instead of asking a person *how* are you, you ask him *who* are you, he is quite surprised. What is the first answer he would give? First, his name, but the name has nothing to do with the person. Then he would say, "I am a doctor. I am a married man. I am the father of two children." These are all qualities which could also be ascribed to a car—it is a four-door sedan, with power steering, and so forth. The car cannot say "I". What a person offers as a description of himself is really a listing of the qualities of an object. Ask him, or ask yourself, who are you, who is that "I"? What is meant when you say, "I feel"? Do *you* really feel, or does *it* feel in you? Do you really feel yourself as the centre of your world, not an egocentric centre but in the sense that you are "original", by which I mean your thoughts and feelings originate in you? If you sit for fifteen or twenty minutes in the morning and try not to think of anything, but to empty your mind, you see how difficult it is for you to be alone with yourself and to have a feeling "this is me".

I want to mention one more point here which refers to the difference between knowing things and knowing man. I can study a corpse or study an organ, and it is a thing. I can use my intellect, and my eyes, of course, too, as well as my machines or gadgets, in order to study this thing. But if I want to know a man, I cannot study him in this way. Of course I can try, and then I will write something about frequency of this-and-that behaviour and about the percentage of this-or-that characteristic. A great deal of the science of psychology is concerned with that, but in this way it is treating man as a thing. The problem the psychiatrist and the psychoanalyst are concerned with, however, the problem we should all be concerned with—to understand our neighbour and ourselves—is to understand a human being who is not a thing. And the process of this understanding cannot be accomplished by the same method by which knowledge in the natural sciences can be accomplished. The knowledge of man is possible *only in the process of relating ourselves to him*. Only if I relate myself to the man whom I want to know, only in the process of relating ourselves to another human being, can we really know something about each other. Ultimate knowledge about another human being cannot be expressed in thought or words—any more than you can explain to someone how Rhine wine tastes. You could explain for a hundred years, but you would never be able to explain how Rhine wine tastes except by drinking it. And you can never exhaust the description of a personality, of a human being, in his full individuality; but you can know him in an act of empathy, in an act of full experience, in an act of love. These are the limitations of scientific psychology, I believe, as far as it aims at the full understanding of human phenomena in word or thought content. It is crucial for the psychiatrist and the psychoanalyst to know that only in this attitude of relatedness can he understand anybody, and I think it is very important for the general physician as well.

The patient, therefore, is to be looked upon as a human being and not just as "that sickness". A doctor is trained in the scientific attitude, in which he observes as one observes in the natural sciences. If he is going to understand his patient, however, and not treat him as a thing, he must learn another attitude which is proper in the science of man: how to relate yourself as one human being to another with utter concentration and utter sincerity. Unless this is done, all slogans about the patient as a person are just so much empty talk.

What, then, are the ethical demands of our day? First of all, to overcome this "thingness"—or, to use a technical term, the "reification" of man; to overcome the concept of ourselves and others as things; to overcome our indifference, our alienation from others, from nature and from ourselves. Second, to arrive again at a new sense of "I-ness", of self, of an experience of "I am", rather than succumb to the automaton feeling in which we have the illusion that "I think what I think", when actually I do not think at all but am rather like someone who puts on a record and thinks that *he* plays the music of the record.

Another aim could be formulated as that of becoming creative. What is creativity? It could mean the ability to create paintings, novels, pictures, works of art, ideas. Of course, that is a matter of learning and of environment, and, I would think, also, of genes; but there is another creativity which is an attitude, a condition behind all creativity in the first sense. Whereas this first kind of creativity is the ability to transmit the creative experience into the material plane, into the creation of something which can be expressed on canvas or otherwise, creativity in the second sense refers to an attitude that can be defined simply: to be aware and to respond. That sounds very simple, and I guess most people would say: "Of course, I am willing to respond." To be aware means to be *really* aware—to be aware of what a person really is, to be aware that a rose is a rose, to speak with Gertrude Stein—to be aware of a tree, to be aware of a scene, and not to be aware of that object as fitting into the *word*-concept tree, which is the way most of us are aware of things.

I will give one example. One day a woman whom I was analyzing came to her appointment very enthusiastically. She had been shelling peas in the kitchen. She told me, "You know, for the first time in my life I experienced that peas roll." Well, we all know that peas roll if they are on the proper surface. We all know that a ball or any round object rolls; but what do we really know? We know in our *minds* that a round object on the proper surface rolls. We see the phenomenon and we state that the facts correspond to what we know; but that is quite different from the creative experience of really *seeing* the movement. Children do that. That is why they can play with a ball again and again and again, because they are not yet bored, because they are not yet *thinking* about it but they are *seeing* it, and it is such a wonderful experience that they can see it again and again and again.

This ability to be aware of a reality of a person, of a tree, of anything, and to respond to that reality, is the essence of creativity. I believe that it is one of the ethical problems of our time to educate men and women and ourselves to be aware and to respond. Another aspect of this is the ability to see; to see man in the act of relatedness, rather than to see him as an object. To put it differently, we must lay the foundations for a new science of man in which man is understood not only with the method of natural science, which is proper in its place and proper also for many fields of anthropology and psychology, but also in the act of love, in the act of empathy, in the act of seeing him man-to-man. Overriding all these aims is to put man back into the saddle, of returning means to means and ends to ends, and to recognize that our achievements in the world of intellect and of material production make sense only if they are means to one end: the full birth of man, as he becomes fully himself, fully human.

Of course, it can easily be said that physicians are part of this culture and society, and suffer from the same defects and the same problems as anybody else. Because of the nature of their work, however, they must relate themselves to their patients; they need to learn not only the method of natural science but also that of the science of man. It is a strange fact that physicians are different; the medical profession is an anachronism with regard to its method of work. I am referring to the difference between artisan production and industrial production. In artisan production as it prevailed in the Middle Ages, one man did his job all by himself. He may have had an assistant or apprentice or somebody who helped him, who cleaned the floor, or planed the wood; but the essential part was done by him. In modern industrial production, we have the opposite. We have the principle which has proved to be so productive of a high degree of division of labour. Nobody makes the whole product; those in charge organize the whole but do not make it. Those who organize do not do the specific work, and those who do the specific work never see the whole. This is the method of industrial production.

The method of work of the doctor is still that of the artisan. He may have a few assistants, he may have this or that gadget, but aside from a few who try to introduce industrial methods into the practice of medicine, most doctors still act like artisans. They are the ones who see the patient and who take the responsibility. In addition, there is another difference. Everybody else today says he works because he wants to earn money. I understand that doctors still claim that this is not really the main reason for their work; that they do their work out of interest for the patient, and earn money only incidentally. The artisan in the Middle Ages had the same attitude. Naturally, he would earn money; but he worked because he loved his work, and many times he would have preferred a smaller income to a more boring type of work. The medical profession again shows itself to be anachronistic, perhaps even less realistic in this respect than in the case of its mode of work.

Now this can have two consequences. It can lend itself to the hypocrisy of claiming ideas which are traditional, which do not quite fit into modern society, without feeling an allegiance to these ideas.

But there is also the possibility that doctors, just because their mode of work is still not so depersonalized, because it is still work in the artisan sense, have greater possibilities than men in any other profession. These possibilities exist provided they recognize their opportunity—to help guide us to a new path of humanism, to a new attitude of understanding of men, which involves the realization by both doctor and patient, that man is not a thing.

7

ON THE LIMITATIONS AND DANGERS OF PSYCHOLOGY

The growing popularity of psychology in our day is greeted by many as a promising sign of our approaching the realization of the Delphic postulate "Know thyself". Undoubtedly there is some reason for this interpretation. The idea of self-knowledge has its roots in the Greek and Judaeo-Christian tradition. It is part of the Enlightenment attitude. James and Freud were deeply rooted in this tradition, and undoubtedly they have helped to transmit this positive aspect of psychology to our present era. But this fact must not lead one to ignore other aspects of the contemporary interest in psychology which are dangerous and destructive to the spiritual development of man. It is with these aspects that the present chapter deals.

Psychological knowledge (*Menschenkenntniss*) has assumed a particular function in capitalist society, a function and a meaning quite different from the meanings implied in "Know thyself".

Capitalistic society is centred around the market—the commodity market and the labour market—where goods and services are exchanged freely regardless of traditional standards and without force of fraud. Instead, knowledge of the customer becomes of paramount importance for the seller. If this was true even fifty or a hundred years ago, the knowledge of the customer has increased in significance a hundredfold in recent decades. With the growing concentration of enterprises and capital, it becomes ever more important to know in advance the wishes of the customer, not only to know them but also to influence and manipulate them. Capital investments on the scale of modern giant enterprises are made not by "hunch", but after thorough investigation and manipulation of the customer. Beyond this knowledge of the customer ("market psychology"), a new field of psychology has arisen based on the wish to understand and manipulate the worker and the employee. This new field is called "human relations". It is a logical outcome of the changed relationship between capital and labour. Instead of crude exploitation there is co-operation between the giant colossi of enterprise and the labour-union bureaucracy, both of whom have come to the conclusion that in the long run it is more useful to arrive at compromises than to fight each other. In addition, however, one has also found that a satisfied, "happy" worker works more productively and contributes to the smooth operation which is a necessity for today's large enterprise. Using the popular interest in psychology and in human relations, the worker and employee are studied and manipulated by psychologists. What Taylor did for the rationalization of physical work, the psychologists are doing for the mental and emotional aspect of the worker. The worker is made into a *thing* and is treated and manipulated like a thing, and the so-called "human relations" are actually the most inhuman ones because they are "reified" and alienated relations.

From the manipulation of the customer and the worker and the employee, the interest of psychology has spread to the manipulation of everybody, as is most clearly expressed in politics. The idea of democracy was originally centred around the concept of clear-thinking and responsible citizens, but in practice, democracy has become more and more influenced by the methods of manipulation which were first developed in market research and human relations.

Though all this is well known, I want now to discuss a more subtle and difficult problem, which is related to the interest in individual psychology, especially to the great popularity of psychoanalysis. The question is: *To what extent is psychology* (the knowledge of others and of oneself) *possible? What limitations exist to such knowledge, and what are the dangers if these limitations are not respected?*

Undoubtedly the desire to know our fellow men and ourselves corresponds to a deep need in human beings. Man lives within a social context. He needs to be related to his fellow man lest he become insane. Man is endowed with reason and imagination. His fellow man and he himself constitute a problem which he cannot help trying to solve, a secret which he must try to discover.

The endeavour to understand man by thought is called "psychology"—"the knowledge of the soul". Psychology, in this sense, attempts to understand the forces underlying man's behaviour, the evolution of man's character, and the circumstances determining this evolution. In short, psychology tries to give a rational account of the innermost core of an individual soul. But complete rational knowledge is possible only of *things*; things can be dissected without being destroyed, they can be manipulated without damage to their very nature, they can be reproduced. *Man is not a thing*; he cannot be dissected without being destroyed, he cannot be manipulated without being harmed, and he cannot be reproduced artificially. While life in its biological aspects is a miracle and a secret, man in his human aspects is an unfathomable secret to himself and to his fellow men. We know our fellow man and ourselves, yet we do not know either him or ourselves—because we are not a thing, and our fellow man is not a thing. The further we reach into the depth of our own being or someone else's being, the more the goal of full knowledge eludes us. Yet we cannot help desiring to penetrate into the secret of man's soul, into the nucleus which is "he".

What, then, is knowing ourselves or knowing another person? Briefly speaking, to know ourselves means to overcome the illusions we have about ourselves; to know our neighbour means to overcome the "parataxic distortions" (transference) we have about him. We all suffer, in varying degrees, from illusions about ourselves. We are enmeshed in phantasies of our omniscience and omnipotence which were experienced as quite real when we were children; we rationalize our bad motivations as being born of benevolence, duty, or necessity; we rationalize our weakness and fear as being in the service of good causes, our unrelatedness as resulting from the unresponsiveness of others. With our fellow man we distort and rationalize just as much, except that usually we do so in the opposite direction. Our lack of love makes him appear as hostile when he is merely shy; our submissiveness transforms him into a dominating ogre when he is simply asserting himself; our fear of spontaneity makes him out to be childish when he is really childlike and spontaneous.

To know more about ourselves means to do away with the many veils that hide us and our neighbour from our view. One veil after another is lifted, one distortion after another dispelled.

Psychology can show us what man is *not*. It cannot tell us what man, each one of us, *is*. The soul of man, the unique core of each individual, can never be grasped and described adequately. It can be "known" only inasmuch as it is not misconceived. The legitimate aim of psychology thus is the *negative*, the removal of distortions and illusions, *not the positive*, the full and complete knowledge of a human being.

There is, however, another path to knowing man's secret; this path is not that of thought but that of *love*. Love is active penetration of the other person, in which the desire to know is stilled by union. (This is love in the biblical meaning of *death* as against *ahaba*.) In the act of fusion I know you, I know myself, I know everybody—and I "know" nothing. I know in the only way in which knowledge of that which is alive is possible for man—by the experience of *union*, not by any knowledge our *thought* can give. The only way to full knowledge lies in the *act* of love; this act transcends thought, it transcends words. It is the daring plunge into the essence of another—or my own.

Psychological knowledge may be a *condition* for full knowledge in the act of love. I have to know the other person and myself objectively in order to be able to see his reality, or, rather, in order to overcome the illusions, the irrationally distorted picture I have of him. If I know a human being as he is, or, rather, if I know what he is not, then I may know him in his ultimate essence, through the act of love.

Love is an achievement not easy to attain. How does the man who cannot love try to penetrate the secret of his neighbour? There is one other way, a desperate one, to get to know the secret: it is that of complete power over another person; the power which makes him do what I want, feel what I want, think what I want; which transforms him into a thing, my thing, my possession. The ultimate degree of this attempt to know lies in the extreme of sadism, in the desire to make a human being suffer, to torture him, to force him to betray his "secret" in his suffering, or eventually to destroy him. In the craving to penetrate man's secret lies an essential motivation for the depth and intensity of cruelty and destructiveness. In a very succinct way this idea has been expressed by the Russian writer Isaac Babel. He quotes a fellow officer in the Russian civil war who had just stamped a former master to death as saying: "With shooting—I'll put it this way—with shooting you only get rid of a chap. . . . With shooting you'll never get at the soul, to where it is in a fellow and how it shows itself. But I don't spare myself, and I've more than once trampled an enemy for over an hour. You see, I want to get to know what life really is, what life's like down our way."[1]

Yet, while sadism and destructiveness are motivated by the desire to force man's secret, this way can never lead to the desired goal. By making my neighbour suffer, the distance between him and myself grows to a point where no knowledge is any longer possible. Sadism and destructiveness are perverted, hopeless, and tragic attempts to know man.[2]

The problem of knowing man is parallel to the theological problem of knowing God. Negative theology postulates that I cannot make any positive statement about God. The only knowledge of God is what He is not. As Maimonides put it, the more I know about what God is not, the more I know about God. Or as Meister Eckhart put it: "Meanwhile man cannot know what God is even though he be ever so well aware of what God is not." One consequence of such negative theology is mysticism. If I can have no full knowledge of God in thought, if theology is at best negative, the positive knowledge of God can be achieved only in the act of union with God.

Translating this principle to the field of man's soul, we might speak of a "negative psychology", and furthermore say that full knowledge of man by thought is impossible, and that full "knowledge" can occur only in the act of love. Just as mysticism is a logical consequence of negative theology, love is the logical consequence of negative psychology.

[1] Isaac Babel, "The Life and Adventures of Matthew Pavlichenko", *The Collected Stories*, Criterion Books, New York, 1955 p. 106.

[2] In children we often see this path to knowledge quite overtly, and as a part of the normal desire of the child to orient himself in a world of physical reality. The child takes something apart and breaks it up in order to know it; or it takes an animal apart; cruelly tears off the wings of a butterfly in order to know it, to force its secret. The apparent cruelty itself is motivated by something deeper: the wish to know the secret of things and of life.

Stating the limitations of psychology is to point to the danger resulting from ignoring these limitations. Modern man is lonely, frightened, and little capable of love. He wants to be close to his neighbour, yet he is too unrelated and distant to be able to be close. His marginal bonds to his neighbour are manifold and easily kept up, but a "central relatedness", that from core to core, hardly exists. In search of closeness he wants knowledge; and in search of knowledge he finds psychology. Psychology becomes a substitute for love, for intimacy, for union with others and oneself; it becomes the refuge for the lonely, alienated man, rather than a step toward the act of union.

This function of psychology as a surrogate becomes apparent in the phenomenon of the popularity of psychoanalysis. Psychoanalysis can be most helpful in undoing the parataxic distortions within ourselves and about our fellow man. It can undo one illusion after another, and thus free the way to the decisive act which we alone can perform: the "courage to be", the jump, the act of ultimate commitment. Man, after his physical birth, has to undergo a continuous process of birth. Emerging from mother's womb is the first stage of birth; from her breast is the second; from her arm, the third. From here on, the process of birth can stop; the person may develop into a socially adjusted and useful person and yet remain stillborn in a spiritual sense. If he is to develop into what he potentially is as a human being, he must continue to be born; that is, he must continue to dissolve the primary ties to soil and blood. He must proceed from one act of separation to the next. He must give up certainty and defences, and take the jump into the act of commitment, concern, and love. What happens so often in psychoanalytic treatment is that there is a silent agreement between therapist and patient, in the assumption that psychoanalysis is a method by which one can attain happiness and maturity and yet avoid the jump, the act, the pain of separation. To carry the analogy of the jump a little further, the psychoanalytic situation looks sometimes like that of a man wanting to learn how to swim, yet being terrified of the moment when he has to jump into the water and have faith in its carrying power. He stands at the edge of the pool and listens as his teacher explains the movements he must make; that is good and necessary; but if we see him going on, talking, listening, talking, we become suspicious that the talking and understanding have become a substitute for the dreaded act. No amount or depth of psychological insight can ever take the place of the act, of the commitment, of the jump. It can lead to it, prepare it, make it possible—and this is the legitimate function of psychoanalytic work. But it must not try to be a substitute for the responsible act of commitment, an act without which no real change occurs in a human being.

If psychoanalysis is understood in this sense, another condition must be met. The analyst must overcome the alienation from himself and from his fellow man which is prevalent in modern man. As I have indicated before, modern man experiences himself as a *thing*, as an embodiment of energies to be invested profitably on the market. He experiences his fellow man as a thing to be used for profitable exchange. Contemporary psychology, psychiatry, and psychoanalysis are involved in this universal process of alienation. The patient is considered as a thing, as the sum of many parts. Some of these parts are defective and need to be repaired, as the parts of an automobile need to be repaired. There is a defect here and a defect there, called symptoms, and the psychiatrist considers it his function to repair or correct these various defects. He does not look at the patient as a global, unique totality which can be fully understood only in the act of full relatedness and empathy. If psychoanalysis is to fulfil its real possibilities, the analyst must overcome his own alienation, must be capable of relating himself to the patient from core to core, and in this relatedness to open the path for the patient's spontaneous experience and thus for the "understanding" of himself. He must not look on the patient as an object, or even only be a "participant observer"; he must become one with him and at the same time retain his separateness and objectivity, so that he can formulate what he experiences in this act of oneness. The final understanding cannot be expressed fully in words; it is not an "interpretation" which describes the patient as an object with its various defects, and their genesis, but it is a global, intuitive grasp; it takes place first in the analyst and then, if the analysis is to be successful, in the patient. This grasp is sudden; it is an intuitive act which can be prepared by many cerebral insights but can never be replaced by them. If psychoanalysis is to develop in this direction, it has, still, unexhausted possibilities for human transformation and spiritual change. If it remains enmeshed in the socially patterned defect of alienation, it may remedy this or that defect, but it will become another tool for making man more automatized and more adjusted to an alienated society.

8

THE PROPHETIC CONCEPT OF PEACE

Even if peace meant only the absence of war, of hate, of slaughter, of madness, its accomplishment would be among the highest aims man can set for himself. But if one wants to understand the *specific prophetic concept of peace*, one has to go several steps further and recognize that the prophetic concept of peace cannot be defined as merely the absence of war, but that it is a spiritual and philosophical concept. It is based on the prophetic idea of man, of history, and of salvation; it has its roots in the story of man's creation and his disobedience to God as related in the Book of Genesis, and it culminates in the concept of the Messianic time.

Before Adam's fall, that is, before man had reason and self-awareness, he lived in complete harmony with nature; "And they were both naked, the man and his wife, and were not ashamed"; they were separate, but they were not aware of it. The first act of disobedience, which is also the beginning of human freedom "opens his eyes", man knows how to judge good and evil, he has become aware of himself and of his fellow man.

Human history has begun. But man is cursed by God for his disobedience.[1]

What is the curse? Enmity and struggle are proclaimed between man and animal ("And I will put enmity between thee [the serpent] and the woman, and between thy seed and her seed; it shall bruise thy head, and thou shalt bruise his heel"), between man and the soil ("Cursed is the ground for thy sake; in sorrow shalt thou eat of it all the days of thy life; thorns also and thistles shall bring it forth to thee; and thou shalt eat the herb of the field, in the sweat of thy face shalt thou eat bread, till thou return unto the ground"), between man and woman ("And thy desire shall be to thy husband, and he shall rule over thee"), between woman and her own natural function ("In sorrow thou shalt bring forth children"). The original, pre-individualist harmony was replaced by conflict and struggle.

Man has to experience himself as a stranger in the world, as estranged from himself and from nature, in order to be able to become one again with himself, with his fellow man, and with nature. He has to experience the split between himself as subject and the world as object as the condition for overcoming this very split. His first sin, disobedience, is the first act of freedom; it is the beginning of human history. It is in history that man develops, evolves, emerges. He develops his reason and his capacity to love. He creates himself in the historical process which began with his first act of freedom, which was the freedom to disobey, to say no.

What is, according to the Old Testament, God's role in this historical process? First and most important, God does not interfere in man's history by an act of grace; he does not change the nature of man; he does not change his heart. (Here lies the basic difference between the prophetic and the Christian concept of salvation.) Man is corrupted because he is estranged, and has not

[1] The word "sin" does not appear in the Biblical text.

overcome his estrangement. But this "corruption" lies in the very nature of human existence, and it is man himself, not God, who can undo the estrangement by achieving new harmony.

God's role in history, according to Old Testament thought, is restricted to sending messengers, the prophets, who (1) show man a new spiritual goal; (2) who show man the alternatives between which he has to choose; and (3) who protest against all acts and attitudes through which man loses himself and the path to salvation. However, man is free to act; it is up to him to decide. He is confronted with the choice between blessing and curse, life and death. It is God's hope that he will choose life, but God does not save man by an act of grace.

This principle is most clearly expressed in the report of God's attitude when the Hebrews ask Samuel to give them a king.

> Then all the elders of Israel gathered together and came to Samuel at Ramah, and said to him, "Behold, you are old and your sons do not walk in your ways; now appoint for us a king to govern us like all the nations." But the thing displeased Samuel when they said, "Give us a king to govern us." And Samuel prayed to the Lord. And the Lord said to Samuel, "Hearken to the voice of the people in all that they say to you; for they have not rejected you, but they have rejected me from being king over them. According to all the deeds which they have done to me, from the day I brought them up out of Egypt even to this day, forsaking me and serving other gods, so they are also doing to you. Now then, hearken to their voice; only, you shall solemnly warn them, and show them the ways of the king who shall reign over them."
>
> So Samuel told all the words of the Lord to the people who were asking a king from him. He said, "These will be the ways of the king who will reign over you: he will take your sons and appoint them to his chariots and to be his horsemen, and to run before his chariots; and he will appoint for himself

> commanders of thousands and commanders of fifties, and some to plough his ground and to reap his harvest, and to make his implements of war and the equipment of his chariots. He will take your daughters to be perfumers and cooks and bakers. He will take the best of your fields and vineyards and olive orchards and give them to his servants. He will take the tenth of your grain and of your vineyards and give it to his officers and to his servants. He will take your manservants and maidservants, and the best of your cattle and your asses, and put them to his work. He will take the tenth of your flocks, and you shall be his slaves. And in that day you will cry out because of your king, whom you have chosen for yourselves; but the Lord will not answer you in that day."
>
> But the people refused to listen to the voice of Samuel; and they said, "No! but we will have a king over us, that we also may be like all the nations, and that our king may govern us and go out before us and fight our battles." And when Samuel had heard all the words of the people, he repeated them in the ears of the Lord. And the Lord said to Samuel, "Hearken to their voice, and make them a king." Samuel then said to the men of Israel, "Go every man to his city" (I *Sam* 8:4–22).

All that Samuel can do is to "hearken to their voice", yet to protest and to show them the consequences of their action. If in spite of this, the people decide for a kingdom, it is their decision and their responsibility.

This principle is also shown quite clearly in the biblical story of the liberation from Egypt. Indeed, God shows Moses how to perform some miracles. These miracles, however, are essentially not different from those the Egyptian magicians could perform. They are clearly meant to give Moses weight in the eyes of Pharaoh and of his own people; they are concessions to Moses because of his fear that the people would not understand his pure message from a nameless God. In the essential point, however, to make the people—or Pharaoh—ready for freedom, God does not interfere at all. Pharaoh remains as he is; hence he becomes worse—his heart "hardens"; the Hebrews do not change either. Again and again they try to escape from freedom, to return to Egyptian slavery and security. God does not change their heart, nor does he change Pharaoh's heart. He lets man alone—lets him make his history, lets him work out his own salvation.

Man's first act of freedom is an act of disobedience; by his act he transcends his original oneness with nature, he becomes aware of himself and of his neighbour, and of their estrangement. In the historical process man creates himself. He grows in self-awareness, in love, in justice, and when he has reached the aim of the full grasp of the world by his own power of reason and love, he has become one again; he has undone the original "sin"; he has returned to paradise, but on the new level of human individualization and independence. Although man has "sinned" in the act of disobedience, his sinning becomes justified in the historical process. He does not suffer from a corruption of his substance, but his very sin is the beginning of a dialectical process which ends with his self-creation and self-salvation.

This completion of his self-creation, the end of the history of strife and conflict and the beginning of a new history of harmony and union, is called the "Messianic time", "the End of the Days", etc. The Messiah is not the saviour. He is not sent by God in order to save the people or to change their corrupt substance. The Messiah is a symbol of man's own achievement. When man has achieved union, when he is ready, then the Messiah will appear. The Messiah is not the Son of God any more than every man is God's child: he is the anointed king who represents the new epoch of history.

The prophetic view of the Messianic time is that of harmony between man and man, man and woman, man and nature. The new harmony is different from that of paradise. It can be obtained only if man develops fully in order to become truly human, if he is capable of loving, if he knows truth and does justice, if he develops his power of reason to a point which frees him from the bondage of man and from the bondage of irrational passions.

The prophetic descriptions abound with symbols of the idea of the new harmony. The earth is undoubtedly fruitful again, swords will be changed into ploughshares, the lion and the lamb will live together in peace, there will be no more war, the whole of mankind will be united in truth and in love.

Peace, in the prophetic vision, is one aspect of the Messianic time; when man has overcome the split that separates him from his fellow men and from nature, then he is indeed at peace with those from whom he was separated. In order to have peace man must find "atonement"; peace is the result of a transformation of man in which union has replaced alienation. Thus the idea of peace, in the prophetic view, cannot be separated from the idea of man's realization of his humanity. Peace is more than a condition of no war; it is harmony and union between men; it is the overcoming of separateness and alienation.

The prophetic concept of peace transcends the realm of human relations; the new harmony is also one between man and nature. Peace between man and nature is *harmony* between man and nature. Man and nature are no longer split; man is not threatened by nature and determined to dominate it: he becomes natural, and nature becomes human. He and nature cease to be opponents and become one. Man is at home in the natural world, and nature becomes part of the human world. This is peace in the prophetic sense. (The Hebrew word for peace, *shalom*, which could be best translated as "completeness", points in the same direction.)

The concept of the Messianic time and of Messianic peace differs, of course, among various prophetic sources. It is not our purpose here to go into the details of such differences. May it suffice to show, with a few characteristic examples, various aspects of the idea of the Messianic time, inasmuch as it is linked with the idea of peace.

The idea of the Messianic time as the state of man's *peace with nature* and the ending of all destructiveness is thus described by Isaiah:

> The wolf shall dwell with the lamb, and the leopard shall lie down with the kid, and the calf and the lion and the fatling together, and a little child shall lead them.
>
> The cow and the bear shall feed; their young shall lie down together; and the lion shall eat straw like the ox.
>
> The suckling child shall play over the hole of an asp, and the weaned child shall put his hand on the adder's den.
>
> They shall not hurt or destroy in all my holy mountain; for the earth shall be full of the knowledge of the Lord as the waters cover the sea (*Isa.* 11:6–9).

The idea of man's new harmony with nature in the Messianic time signifies not only the end of the struggle of man against nature but also that nature will not withhold itself from man—it will become the all-loving, nursing mother. Nature within man will cease to be crippled, and nature outside man will cease to be sterile. As Isaiah put it:

> Then the eyes of the blind shall be opened, and the ears of the deaf unstopped;
>
> Then shall the lame man leap like a hart, and the tongue of the dumb sing for joy. For waters shall break forth in the wilderness, and streams in the desert;
>
> The burning sand shall become a pool, and the thirsty ground springs of water; the haunt of jackals shall become a swamp, the grass shall become reeds and rushes.
>
> And a highway shall be there, and it shall be called the Holy

> Way; the unclean shall not pass over it, and fools shall not err therein.
>
> No lion shall be there, nor shall any ravenous beast come up on it. They shall not be found there, but the redeemed shall walk there.
>
> And the ransomed of the Lord shall return, and come to Zion with singing; everlasting joy shall be upon their heads; they shall obtain joy and gladness, and sorrow and sighing shall flee away (*Isa.* 35:5–10).

Or, as the second Isaiah puts it:

> Behold, I am doing a new thing; now it springs forth, do you not perceive it? I will make a way in the wilderness and rivers in the desert.
>
> The wild beasts will honour me, the jackals and the ostriches; for I give water in the wilderness, rivers in the desert, to give drink to my chosen people (*Isa.* 43:19–20).

The idea of the new union between man and man in which their estrangement and destructiveness have disappeared is expressed by Micah:

> He shall judge between many peoples, and shall decide for strong nations afar off; and they shall beat their swords into ploughshares, and their spears into pruning hooks; nation shall not lift up sword against nation, neither shall they learn war any more;
>
> But they shall sit every man under his vine and under his fig tree, and none shall make them afraid; for the mouth of the Lord of hosts has spoken.
>
> For all the peoples walk each in the name of its god, but we will walk in the name of the Lord our God for ever and ever (*Micah* 4:3–5).

But, in the Messianic concept man will not only cease to destroy man. He will have overcome the experience of separateness between one nation and another. Once he has achieved being fully human, the stranger ceases to be a stranger; the illusion of the difference between nation and nation disappears, there are no longer any chosen peoples, just as they will not even have to worship the same god, since the conceptual concept of God is itself an illusion. As Amos puts it:

> "Are you not like the Ethiopians to me, O people of Israel?" says the Lord. "Did I not bring up Israel from the land of Egypt, and the Philistines from Caphtor and the Syrians from Kir?" (*Amos* 9:7).

The same idea that all nations are equally loved by God and that there is no more favourite son is beautifully expressed also by Isaiah:

> In that day there will be a highway from Egypt to Assyria, and the Assyrian will come into Egypt, and the Egyptian into Assyria, and the Egyptians will worship with the Assyrians.
>
> In that day Israel will be the third with Egypt and Assyria, a blessing in the midst of the earth, whom the Lord of hosts has blessed, saying, "Blessed be Egypt my people, and Assyria the work of my hands, and Israel my heritage" (*Isa.* 19:23–24).

To sum up, the prophetic idea of peace is part of the prophets' whole historical and religious concept which culminates in their idea of the Messianic time; peace between man and man and between man and nature is more than absence of strife; it is the accomplishment of true harmony and union; it is the experience of "at-onement" with the world and within oneself; it is the end of alienation, the return of man to himself.

Index